Liberalism: A Very Short Introduction

VERY SHORT INTRODUCTIONS are for anyone wanting a stimulating and accessible way into a new subject. They are written by experts, and have been translated into more than 40 different languages.

The series began in 1995, and now covers a wide variety of topics in every discipline. The VSI library now contains over 350 volumes—a Very Short Introduction to everything from Psychology and Philosophy of Science to American History and Relativity—and continues to grow in every subject area.

Very Short Introductions available now:

ACCOUNTING Christopher Nobes
ADVERTISING Winston Fletcher
AFRICAN AMERICAN RELIGION Eddie S. Glaude Jr.
AFRICAN HISTORY John Parker and Richard Rathbone
AFRICAN RELIGIONS Jacob K. Olupona
AGNOSTICISM Robin Le Poidevin
ALEXANDER THE GREAT Hugh Bowden
AMERICAN HISTORY Paul S. Boyer
AMERICAN IMMIGRATION David A. Gerber
AMERICAN LEGAL HISTORY G. Edward White
AMERICAN POLITICAL HISTORY Donald Critchlow
AMERICAN POLITICAL PARTIES AND ELECTIONS L. Sandy Maisel
AMERICAN POLITICS Richard M. Valelly
THE AMERICAN PRESIDENCY Charles O. Jones
AMERICAN SLAVERY Heather Andrea Williams
THE AMERICAN WEST Stephen Aron
AMERICAN WOMEN'S HISTORY Susan Ware
ANAESTHESIA Aidan O'Donnell
ANARCHISM Colin Ward
ANCIENT ASSYRIA Karen Radner
ANCIENT EGYPT Ian Shaw
ANCIENT EGYPTIAN ART AND ARCHITECTURE Christina Riggs
ANCIENT GREECE Paul Cartledge
THE ANCIENT NEAR EAST Amanda H. Podany
ANCIENT PHILOSOPHY Julia Annas
ANCIENT WARFARE Harry Sidebottom
ANGELS David Albert Jones
ANGLICANISM Mark Chapman
THE ANGLO-SAXON AGE John Blair
THE ANIMAL KINGDOM Peter Holland
ANIMAL RIGHTS David DeGrazia
THE ANTARCTIC Klaus Dodds
ANTISEMITISM Steven Beller
ANXIETY Daniel Freeman and Jason Freeman
THE APOCRYPHAL GOSPELS Paul Foster
ARCHAEOLOGY Paul Bahn
ARCHITECTURE Andrew Ballantyne
ARISTOCRACY William Doyle
ARISTOTLE Jonathan Barnes
ART HISTORY Dana Arnold
ART THEORY Cynthia Freeland
ASTROBIOLOGY David C. Catling
ATHEISM Julian Baggini
AUGUSTINE Henry Chadwick
AUSTRALIA Kenneth Morgan
AUTISM Uta Frith
THE AVANT GARDE David Cottington
THE AZTECS Davíd Carrasco
BACTERIA Sebastian G. B. Amyes
BARTHES Jonathan Culler
THE BEATS David Sterritt
BEAUTY Roger Scruton
BESTSELLERS John Sutherland

THE BIBLE John Riches
BIBLICAL ARCHAEOLOGY Eric H. Cline
BIOGRAPHY Hermione Lee
THE BLUES Elijah Wald
THE BOOK OF MORMON Terryl Givens
BORDERS Alexander C. Diener and Joshua Hagen
THE BRAIN Michael O'Shea
THE BRITISH CONSTITUTION Martin Loughlin
THE BRITISH EMPIRE Ashley Jackson
BRITISH POLITICS Anthony Wright
BUDDHA Michael Carrithers
BUDDHISM Damien Keown
BUDDHIST ETHICS Damien Keown
CANCER Nicholas James
CAPITALISM James Fulcher
CATHOLICISM Gerald O'Collins
CAUSATION Stephen Mumford and Rani Lill Anjum
THE CELL Terence Allen and Graham Cowling
THE CELTS Barry Cunliffe
CHAOS Leonard Smith
CHEMISTRY Peter Atkins
CHILD PSYCHOLOGY Usha Goswami
CHILDREN'S LITERATURE Kimberley Reynolds
CHINESE LITERATURE Sabina Knight
CHOICE THEORY Michael Allingham
CHRISTIAN ART Beth Williamson
CHRISTIAN ETHICS D. Stephen Long
CHRISTIANITY Linda Woodhead
CITIZENSHIP Richard Bellamy
CIVIL ENGINEERING David Muir Wood
CLASSICAL LITERATURE William Allan
CLASSICAL MYTHOLOGY Helen Morales
CLASSICS Mary Beard and John Henderson
CLAUSEWITZ Michael Howard
CLIMATE Mark Maslin
THE COLD WAR Robert McMahon
COLONIAL AMERICA Alan Taylor
COLONIAL LATIN AMERICAN LITERATURE Rolena Adorno
COMEDY Matthew Bevis
COMMUNISM Leslie Holmes
COMPLEXITY John H. Holland
THE COMPUTER Darrel Ince
CONFUCIANISM Daniel K. Gardner
THE CONQUISTADORS Matthew Restall and Felipe Fernández-Armesto
CONSCIENCE Paul Strohm
CONSCIOUSNESS Susan Blackmore
CONTEMPORARY ART Julian Stallabrass
CONTEMPORARY FICTION Robert Eaglestone
CONTINENTAL PHILOSOPHY Simon Critchley
CORAL REEFS Charles Sheppard
CORPORATE SOCIAL RESPONSIBILITY Jeremy Moon
CORRUPTION Leslie Holmes
COSMOLOGY Peter Coles
CRIME FICTION Richard Bradford
CRITICAL THEORY Stephen Eric Bronner
THE CRUSADES Christopher Tyerman
CRYPTOGRAPHY Fred Piper and Sean Murphy
THE CULTURAL REVOLUTION Richard Curt Kraus
DADA AND SURREALISM David Hopkins
DANTE Peter Hainsworth and David Robey
DARWIN Jonathan Howard
THE DEAD SEA SCROLLS Timothy Lim
DEMOCRACY Bernard Crick
DERRIDA Simon Glendinning
DESCARTES Tom Sorell
DESERTS Nick Middleton
DESIGN John Heskett
DEVELOPMENTAL BIOLOGY Lewis Wolpert
THE DEVIL Darren Oldridge
DIASPORA Kevin Kenny
DICTIONARIES Lynda Mugglestone
DINOSAURS David Norman
DIPLOMACY Joseph M. Siracusa
DOCUMENTARY FILM Patricia Aufderheide
DREAMING J. Allan Hobson
DRUGS Leslie Iversen
DRUIDS Barry Cunliffe
EARLY MUSIC Thomas Forrest Kelly
THE EARTH Martin Redfern
ECONOMICS Partha Dasgupta

EDUCATION Gary Thomas
EGYPTIAN MYTH Geraldine Pinch
EIGHTEENTH-CENTURY BRITAIN Paul Langford
THE ELEMENTS Philip Ball
EMOTION Dylan Evans
EMPIRE Stephen Howe
ENGELS Terrell Carver
ENGINEERING David Blockley
ENGLISH LITERATURE Jonathan Bate
ENTREPRENEURSHIP Paul Westhead and Mike Wright
ENVIRONMENTAL ECONOMICS Stephen Smith
EPIDEMIOLOGY Rodolfo Saracci
ETHICS Simon Blackburn
ETHNOMUSICOLOGY Timothy Rice
THE ETRUSCANS Christopher Smith
THE EUROPEAN UNION John Pinder and Simon Usherwood
EVOLUTION Brian and Deborah Charlesworth
EXISTENTIALISM Thomas Flynn
EXPLORATION Stewart A. Weaver
THE EYE Michael Land
FAMILY LAW Jonathan Herring
FASCISM Kevin Passmore
FASHION Rebecca Arnold
FEMINISM Margaret Walters
FILM Michael Wood
FILM MUSIC Kathryn Kalinak
THE FIRST WORLD WAR Michael Howard
FOLK MUSIC Mark Slobin
FOOD John Krebs
FORENSIC PSYCHOLOGY David Canter
FORENSIC SCIENCE Jim Fraser
FORESTS Jaboury Ghazoul
FOSSILS Keith Thomson
FOUCAULT Gary Gutting
FRACTALS Kenneth Falconer
FREE SPEECH Nigel Warburton
FREE WILL Thomas Pink
FRENCH LITERATURE John D. Lyons
THE FRENCH REVOLUTION William Doyle
FREUD Anthony Storr
FUNDAMENTALISM Malise Ruthven
GALAXIES John Gribbin
GALILEO Stillman Drake
GAME THEORY Ken Binmore
GANDHI Bhikhu Parekh
GENES Jonathan Slack
GENIUS Andrew Robinson
GEOGRAPHY John Matthews and David Herbert
GEOPOLITICS Klaus Dodds
GERMAN LITERATURE Nicholas Boyle
GERMAN PHILOSOPHY Andrew Bowie
GLOBAL CATASTROPHES Bill McGuire
GLOBAL ECONOMIC HISTORY Robert C. Allen
GLOBALIZATION Manfred Steger
GOD John Bowker
THE GOTHIC Nick Groom
GOVERNANCE Mark Bevir
THE GREAT DEPRESSION AND THE NEW DEAL Eric Rauchway
HABERMAS James Gordon Finlayson
HAPPINESS Daniel M. Haybron
HEGEL Peter Singer
HEIDEGGER Michael Inwood
HERODOTUS Jennifer T. Roberts
HIEROGLYPHS Penelope Wilson
HINDUISM Kim Knott
HISTORY John H. Arnold
THE HISTORY OF ASTRONOMY Michael Hoskin
THE HISTORY OF LIFE Michael Benton
THE HISTORY OF MATHEMATICS Jacqueline Stedall
THE HISTORY OF MEDICINE William Bynum
THE HISTORY OF TIME Leofranc Holford-Strevens
HIV/AIDS Alan Whiteside
HOBBES Richard Tuck
HORMONES Martin Luck
HUMAN ANATOMY Leslie Klenerman
HUMAN EVOLUTION Bernard Wood
HUMAN RIGHTS Andrew Clapham
HUMANISM Stephen Law
HUME A. J. Ayer
HUMOUR Noël Carroll
THE ICE AGE Jamie Woodward
IDEOLOGY Michael Freeden
INDIAN PHILOSOPHY Sue Hamilton
INFECTIOUS DISEASE Marta L. Wayne and Benjamin M. Bolker

INFORMATION Luciano Floridi
INNOVATION Mark Dodgson and David Gann
INTELLIGENCE Ian J. Deary
INTERNATIONAL MIGRATION Khalid Koser
INTERNATIONAL RELATIONS Paul Wilkinson
INTERNATIONAL SECURITY Christopher S. Browning
IRAN Ali M. Ansari
ISLAM Malise Ruthven
ISLAMIC HISTORY Adam Silverstein
ITALIAN LITERATURE Peter Hainsworth and David Robey
JESUS Richard Bauckham
JOURNALISM Ian Hargreaves
JUDAISM Norman Solomon
JUNG Anthony Stevens
KABBALAH Joseph Dan
KAFKA Ritchie Robertson
KANT Roger Scruton
KEYNES Robert Skidelsky
KIERKEGAARD Patrick Gardiner
KNOWLEDGE Jennifer Nagel
THE KORAN Michael Cook
LANDSCAPE ARCHITECTURE Ian H. Thompson
LANDSCAPES AND GEOMORPHOLOGY Andrew Goudie and Heather Viles
LANGUAGES Stephen R. Anderson
LATE ANTIQUITY Gillian Clark
LAW Raymond Wacks
THE LAWS OF THERMODYNAMICS Peter Atkins
LEADERSHIP Keith Grint
LIBERALISM Michael Freeden
LINCOLN Allen C. Guelzo
LINGUISTICS Peter Matthews
LITERARY THEORY Jonathan Culler
LOCKE John Dunn
LOGIC Graham Priest
LOVE Ronald de Sousa
MACHIAVELLI Quentin Skinner
MADNESS Andrew Scull
MAGIC Owen Davies
MAGNA CARTA Nicholas Vincent
MAGNETISM Stephen Blundell
MALTHUS Donald Winch
MANAGEMENT John Hendry
MAO Delia Davin
MARINE BIOLOGY Philip V. Mladenov
THE MARQUIS DE SADE John Phillips
MARTIN LUTHER Scott H. Hendrix
MARTYRDOM Jolyon Mitchell
MARX Peter Singer
MATERIALS Christopher Hall
MATHEMATICS Timothy Gowers
THE MEANING OF LIFE Terry Eagleton
MEDICAL ETHICS Tony Hope
MEDICAL LAW Charles Foster
MEDIEVAL BRITAIN John Gillingham and Ralph A. Griffiths
MEMORY Jonathan K. Foster
METAPHYSICS Stephen Mumford
MICHAEL FARADAY Frank A. J. L. James
MICROBIOLOGY Nicholas P. Money
MICROECONOMICS Avinash Dixit
MICROSCOPY Terence Allen
THE MIDDLE AGES Miri Rubin
MINERALS David Vaughan
MODERN ART David Cottington
MODERN CHINA Rana Mitter
MODERN FRANCE Vanessa R. Schwartz
MODERN IRELAND Senia Pašeta
MODERN JAPAN Christopher Goto-Jones
MODERN LATIN AMERICAN LITERATURE Roberto González Echevarría
MODERN WAR Richard English
MODERNISM Christopher Butler
MOLECULES Philip Ball
THE MONGOLS Morris Rossabi
MORMONISM Richard Lyman Bushman
MUHAMMAD Jonathan A. C. Brown
MULTICULTURALISM Ali Rattansi
MUSIC Nicholas Cook
MYTH Robert A. Segal
THE NAPOLEONIC WARS Mike Rapport
NATIONALISM Steven Grosby
NELSON MANDELA Elleke Boehmer
NEOLIBERALISM Manfred Steger and Ravi Roy
NETWORKS Guido Caldarelli and Michele Catanzaro

THE NEW TESTAMENT Luke Timothy Johnson
THE NEW TESTAMENT AS LITERATURE Kyle Keefer
NEWTON Robert Iliffe
NIETZSCHE Michael Tanner
NINETEENTH-CENTURY BRITAIN Christopher Harvie and H. C. G. Matthew
THE NORMAN CONQUEST George Garnett
NORTH AMERICAN INDIANS Theda Perdue and Michael D. Green
NORTHERN IRELAND Marc Mulholland
NOTHING Frank Close
NUCLEAR POWER Maxwell Irvine
NUCLEAR WEAPONS Joseph M. Siracusa
NUMBERS Peter M. Higgins
NUTRITION David A. Bender
OBJECTIVITY Stephen Gaukroger
THE OLD TESTAMENT Michael D. Coogan
THE ORCHESTRA D. Kern Holoman
ORGANIZATIONS Mary Jo Hatch
PAGANISM Owen Davies
THE PALESTINIAN-ISRAELI CONFLICT Martin Bunton
PARTICLE PHYSICS Frank Close
PAUL E. P. Sanders
PEACE Oliver P. Richmond
PENTECOSTALISM William K. Kay
THE PERIODIC TABLE Eric R. Scerri
PHILOSOPHY Edward Craig
PHILOSOPHY OF LAW Raymond Wacks
PHILOSOPHY OF SCIENCE Samir Okasha
PHOTOGRAPHY Steve Edwards
PHYSICAL CHEMISTRY Peter Atkins
PILGRIMAGE Ian Reader
PLAGUE Paul Slack
PLANETS David A. Rothery
PLANTS Timothy Walker
PLATE TECTONICS Peter Molnar
PLATO Julia Annas
POLITICAL PHILOSOPHY David Miller
POLITICS Kenneth Minogue
POSTCOLONIALISM Robert Young
POSTMODERNISM Christopher Butler
POSTSTRUCTURALISM Catherine Belsey
PREHISTORY Chris Gosden
PRESOCRATIC PHILOSOPHY Catherine Osborne
PRIVACY Raymond Wacks
PROBABILITY John Haigh
PROGRESSIVISM Walter Nugent
PROTESTANTISM Mark A. Noll
PSYCHIATRY Tom Burns
PSYCHOLOGY Gillian Butler and Freda McManus
PSYCHOTHERAPY Tom Burns and Eva Burns-Lundgren
PURITANISM Francis J. Bremer
THE QUAKERS Pink Dandelion
QUANTUM THEORY John Polkinghorne
RACISM Ali Rattansi
RADIOACTIVITY Claudio Tuniz
RASTAFARI Ennis B. Edmonds
THE REAGAN REVOLUTION Gil Troy
REALITY Jan Westerhoff
THE REFORMATION Peter Marshall
RELATIVITY Russell Stannard
RELIGION IN AMERICA Timothy Beal
THE RENAISSANCE Jerry Brotton
RENAISSANCE ART Geraldine A. Johnson
REVOLUTIONS Jack A. Goldstone
RHETORIC Richard Toye
RISK Baruch Fischhoff and John Kadvany
RITUAL Barry Stephenson
RIVERS Nick Middleton
ROBOTICS Alan Winfield
ROMAN BRITAIN Peter Salway
THE ROMAN EMPIRE Christopher Kelly
THE ROMAN REPUBLIC David M. Gwynn
ROMANTICISM Michael Ferber
ROUSSEAU Robert Wokler
RUSSELL A. C. Grayling
RUSSIAN HISTORY Geoffrey Hosking
RUSSIAN LITERATURE Catriona Kelly
THE RUSSIAN REVOLUTION S. A. Smith
SCHIZOPHRENIA Chris Frith and Eve Johnstone

SCHOPENHAUER Christopher Janaway
SCIENCE AND RELIGION
Thomas Dixon
SCIENCE FICTION David Seed
THE SCIENTIFIC REVOLUTION
Lawrence M. Principe
SCOTLAND Rab Houston
SEXUALITY Véronique Mottier
SIKHISM Eleanor Nesbitt
THE SILK ROAD James A. Millward
SLEEP Steven W. Lockley and
Russell G. Foster
SOCIAL AND CULTURAL
ANTHROPOLOGY
John Monaghan and Peter Just
SOCIAL WORK Sally Holland and
Jonathan Scourfield
SOCIALISM Michael Newman
SOCIOLINGUISTICS John Edwards
SOCIOLOGY Steve Bruce
SOCRATES C. C. W. Taylor
THE SOVIET UNION Stephen Lovell
THE SPANISH CIVIL WAR
Helen Graham
SPANISH LITERATURE Jo Labanyi
SPINOZA Roger Scruton
SPIRITUALITY Philip Sheldrake
SPORT Mike Cronin
STARS Andrew King
STATISTICS David J. Hand
STEM CELLS Jonathan Slack
STRUCTURAL ENGINEERING
David Blockley
STUART BRITAIN John Morrill
SUPERCONDUCTIVITY
Stephen Blundell
SYMMETRY Ian Stewart
TAXATION Stephen Smith
TEETH Peter S. Ungar
TERRORISM Charles Townshend
THEATRE Marvin Carlson
THEOLOGY David F. Ford
THOMAS AQUINAS Fergus Kerr
THOUGHT Tim Bayne
TIBETAN BUDDHISM
Matthew T. Kapstein
TOCQUEVILLE Harvey C. Mansfield
TRAGEDY Adrian Poole
THE TROJAN WAR Eric H. Cline
TRUST Katherine Hawley
THE TUDORS John Guy
TWENTIETH-CENTURY
BRITAIN Kenneth O. Morgan
THE UNITED NATIONS
Jussi M. Hanhimäki
THE U.S. CONGRESS Donald A. Ritchie
THE U.S. SUPREME COURT
Linda Greenhouse
UTOPIANISM Lyman Tower Sargent
THE VIKINGS Julian Richards
VIRUSES Dorothy H. Crawford
WILLIAM SHAKESPEARE
Stanley Wells
WITCHCRAFT Malcolm Gaskill
WITTGENSTEIN A. C. Grayling
WORK Stephen Fineman
WORLD MUSIC Philip Bohlman
THE WORLD TRADE ORGANIZATION
Amrita Narlikar
WORLD WAR II Gerhard L. Weinberg
WRITING AND SCRIPT
Andrew Robinson

Available soon:

PSYCHOANALYSIS Daniel Pick
NUCLEAR PHYSICS Frank Close
SOCIAL PSYCHOLOGY Richard J. Crisp
BYZANTIUM Peter Sarris
WATER John Finney

For more information visit our website

www.oup.com/vsi/

Michael Freeden

LIBERALISM

A Very Short Introduction

UNIVERSITY PRESS

Great Clarendon Street, Oxford, OX2 6DP,
United Kingdom

Oxford University Press is a department of the University of Oxford.
It furthers the University's objective of excellence in research, scholarship,
and education by publishing worldwide. Oxford is a registered trade mark of
Oxford University Press in the UK and in certain other countries

First edition published in 2015

Impression: 1

Published in the United States of America by Oxford University Press
198 Madison Avenue, New York, NY 10016, United States of America

British Library Cataloguing in Publication Data
Data available

Library of Congress Control Number: 2014959958

ISBN 978-0-19-967043-7

Printed in Great Britain by
Ashford Colour Press Ltd, Gosport, Hampshire

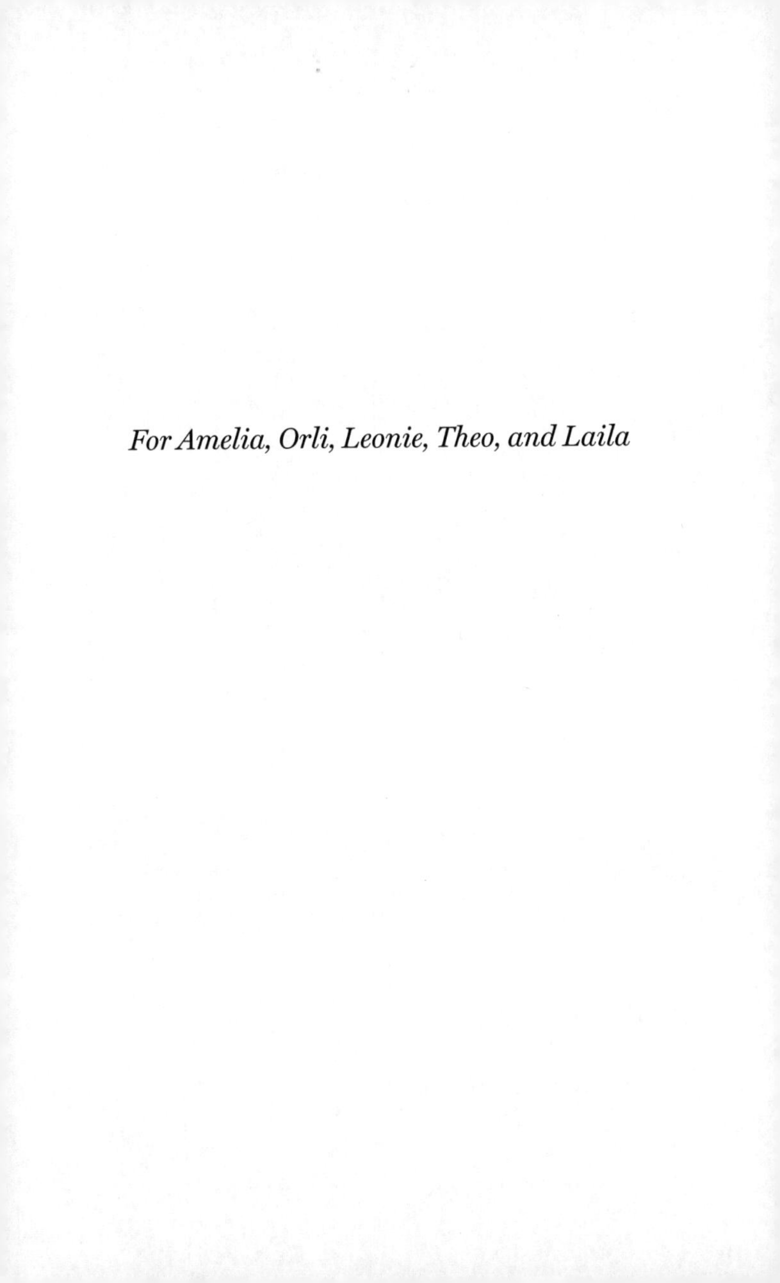

For Amelia, Orli, Leonie, Theo, and Laila

Contents

List of illustrations

Chapter 1
A house of many mansions

When people first used the word 'liberal' as generous or ample they had little idea of the mighty current liberalism was to unleash. Some indication of its future life emerged when 'liberal' became associated with open-mindedness and tolerance. But ever since the term 'liberales' was coined in Spain two hundred years ago to represent a political party, liberalism has been positioned squarely on the public stage: as a rallying cry for individuals desiring space to be free from unjustifiable limitations, and as a set of fundamental institutional arrangements meant to legitimate and civilize the practices of politics. Above all it has become indicative of ideas and policies intended to reform, to emancipate, and to open up possibilities for individuals wishing to live their lives according to their own understandings. Like all ideologies and collectively held belief systems, liberalism competes over public recognition and implementation, and like all of them it has also been decried from numerous quarters.

Yet the problem is this: There is no single, unambiguous thing called liberalism. All the liberalisms that have existed, and that exist, select—deliberately or unconsciously—certain items from an accumulated and crowded liberal repertoire and leave others out, both because some elements are incompatible with others and because intellectual fashions and practices change. As a consequence, a host of belief systems and theories nest under the heading liberalism, none of which can contain all the possibilities—the ideas and the political arrangements—that the term in its maximal but hypothetical fullness can encompass, or that liberal political practices have encompassed over time and across space. Consider for example phrases such as classical liberalism, social liberalism, or neoliberalism: three versions that are still current today. Classical liberalism revolved around individual liberty (the close etymological relation of liberalism), human independence, and the rule of law, and it importantly restricted what states and governments were entitled to do to individuals. Social liberalism—and the new liberalism that emerged in Britain just over a century ago, in tandem with some of its Scandinavian social-democratic counterparts—explored the conditions for individual development and growth, sustained by networks of mutual assistance and interdependence. From that branch of liberalism arose the modern welfare state. However, in a particularly confusing way, 'neo' and 'new' pull in very different directions. Neoliberalism—a product mainly of the second half of the 20th century—emphasizes the beneficial consequences of competitive markets and personal advancement far more than the general nourishing of human well-being. Its liberal credentials are highly contentious, as will be argued in Chapter 7. Those who think that liberalism is largely about unrestrained private activity and those who believe liberalism is about the reasonable development of individuals in a mutually supporting and project-sharing society do not have too much in common.

No less strikingly, there is often disagreement over which of liberalism's features is the most important, a disagreement evident among both liberals and their critics. Is liberalism about the increase of individual liberty or about treating everyone with equal respect? Is it about limiting harm to others or about enabling human flourishing? Is it about being more humane or more productive? Is there one true liberalism surrounded by shadowy

1. This word cloud represents some of the diversity and internal complexity of the ideas comprising liberalism and from which different liberalisms may be fashioned. Even then, it does not include privacy and property, which many believe are also integral to liberalism.

imitations? Have other ideologies pecked away at liberalism like vultures, carrying off some of its choice parts but leaving the rest to shrivel? The challenge for the student of liberalism is to make sense of these different understandings rather than to express a rigid preference for one of them. It may therefore be more accurate to talk about *liberalisms* in the plural, all part of a broad family exhibiting both similarities and differences (Figure 1). Many members of the liberal family overlap in their characteristics, but some are hardly on speaking terms.

Has liberalism triumphed?

Both as a political-ideological creed and as a philosophical reflection on the features of a just society, countless liberal enthusiasts regard it as a great success story. One of their most ardent voices has been that of Francis Fukuyama, an American philosopher who, over twenty years ago, announced the victory of the 'liberal idea'. Liberalism, in his view, had become universally accepted, and no other ideology could make a similar claim to such universality. Was that then the end of ideological conflict? Were we all liberals now? Three problems with that confident view immediately come to mind. First, where is the finishing post of an ideology positioned? When does an ideology cross the line and breathe with relief: 'we've finally beaten the others!'? History offers little indication of such finality, particularly when we judge present events and ideas. After all, even a belief in magic—once a powerful factor in interpreting what happens in the world—has not entirely disappeared in modern societies. Unless we know what the criterion of an ideological victory is, and unless we can establish a clear end to ideological clashes, the question remains meaningless. In effect, those who assume the victory of liberalism merely assert uncritically that one version of liberalism has won and the others have lost. That, too, must remain unsubstantiated, for what counts as victory in the field of ideas, theory, or ideology will always be contested. Short-term victories may well end up as long-term defeats: the history of 20th century communism attests to that, but who knows what may happen to communism's fortunes in the even longer term?

Second, there is scant evidence that liberalism has been accepted in most parts of the globe. Side-by-side with aspirations to some kind of liberal democracy we encounter ideologies based on religion, forms of radical populism, autocratic states of belief and rule, and, of course, many conservative regimes. In Fukuyama's own society, in the USA, a considerable amount of invective is piled up against liberalism. But is there nonetheless a process of growing convergence on liberal points of view? Well, it seems premature and wrong-headed to pass judgement on the future spread of other ideologies. Predicting the future of ideas has become more, not less, difficult in a fast-changing and increasingly fragmented world. Even those who claim to witness a move towards growing globalization may be talking about competing visions of globalism that differ markedly from one another: for instance, a globalization of market values as against a globalization of human solidarity. So the globalization of liberalism is still a glint in someone's eye, and it may never happen.

Third, Fukuyama implied that there was one clear thing called liberalism. The evidence suggests otherwise. We can be greatly assisted in understanding liberalism by recognizing that there are various ways of looking at it. Each perspective will illuminate some of its features while obscuring others. When we look at a painting, we may ask questions about the artist, about its composition, about its aesthetics, about the techniques and materials used, about its commercial value, or about its place in the history of art. It all depends on which subject interests us most. Similarly, with liberalism as with all ideologies, there is no distinct approach that will tell us all we want to know about it, no easy single definition that will cover all its manifestations.

This book will therefore explore liberalism from a number of angles. Using Fukuyama's flawed metaphor, there are many liberal runners in that so-called race, so even were we impetuously to declare liberalism a winner, this would not reveal which of liberalism's many versions has 'won'. The ideas and arrangements nesting under the label 'liberalism' may mutate significantly, as indeed they already have done in the past. The frequent bouts of 'endism' that afflict political commentators as well as social prophets exude more than a whiff of utopianism, of teleological inevitability, or perhaps even cynicism. Yet even though no definition of liberalism can include all its varieties, its more durable features will be spelt out in Chapter 4.

The seductiveness of liberalism

There is something about liberalism that many people find very attractive. Although liberalism falls short of the final universalism attributed to it by Fukuyama, a large number of political philosophers nonetheless regard it as a noble vision of social and political life that should be extended to all. Failing even that, liberalism is a widely revered set of ideas, at least in the Western world—though, as we shall see, it is also deplored both by radicals and by conservatives. Moreover, liberal practices on the ground have institutional consequences, and those consequences are woven into a grand—and sometimes self-congratulatory—historical tapestry. Many of those practices are contained in the phrase 'liberal democracy'. As a principle of good government, liberal democracy has firm roots in numerous countries and is an aspirational goal in others. It has a clear message: democracy, if by that we mean the rule of the people, is all well and good, but winning elections and popular government on their own are merely a minimum kit. That kit is necessary but insufficient for a political system to be called 'liberal'. Liberals maintain that democracy must display additional characteristics for it to be considered a worthy system of government. Democracy needs to be fair, tolerant, inclusive, restrained, and self-critical, not simply the pursuit of majority rule. Liberal democracy involves not just elections, but free elections. It involves not just representative government, but accountable and constrained government. It involves not just the right to vote, but the equal and unsupervised right to vote. And it involves attention to the well-being of all the members of a society, a principle that requires some governmental activity but may be open to different interpretations. The qualities liberals demand are extensive and varied: it is a lot easier to preach liberalism than to realize it.

Liberal practices affect constitutions, the degree of openness permitted in political debate, and the basket of rights that societies are willing to distribute among their members. Often, too, they involve ambitious schemes of redistributing wealth to increase the life chances of all, although some commentators, usually from a conservative or libertarian perspective, might deplore that as a form of socialism. And, as usually is the case with any ideology, a gap may open up between declared principles and effective practice. Liberal principles may be breached even by those subscribing to them, and some societies reject them out of hand. In that case, we may have to decide whether liberal principles or liberal practices bring us closer to identifying what is typical of liberalism. Assessing liberalism is not an armchair intellectual activity—though there is nothing wrong with that. It relates rather to what kind of politics a society engages in at the coalface.

But there also are liberal frames of mind, liberal patterns of thinking that operate in the world of political discourse, language, and disputation. Philosophers, political theorists, historians of ideas, practising politicians, and political parties all weigh in with their disparate models, objectives, critiques, and certainties. As a set of guiding principles for leading the good life, liberalism is frequently understood by philosophers and ethicists to be a binding set of virtues and precepts that deserves universal standing. So while Fukuyama regarded liberalism as a universal ideology, which it plainly is not, a number of political theorists nonetheless hold that liberalism is a philosophical and ethical imperative that ought to be universal: the highest expression of norms of social morality and justice. For them it exists as a general set of ideals appropriate for all right-thinking individuals, regardless of whether or not it is realized in actuality. In sum, for many, liberalism is a label keenly pursued and, when attained, staunchly defended. Its supporters bask in the light of the term; its detractors pour scorn on its unworldliness or hypocrisy.

A plethora of particular liberalisms

There is another issue at stake. Liberalism originated out of a European set of beliefs, but it does not have an agreed meaning, even on that one continent. Within Europe its reputation, and the connotations it arouses, have located it on very different points of the political spectrum: left of centre in the United Kingdom, right of centre in France and Germany. In Scandinavian countries, particularly in Sweden, many liberal ideas have been disseminated under the heading of social-democracy, while what is labelled as liberalism there has frequently been linked to elitist or middle class individualism. In much of Europe and beyond, socialists of all stripes have accused liberalism of acting against the interests of the working classes and of furthering anti-social selfishness, defying the message of inclusiveness that many liberals wish to spread. In Eastern Europe since the fall of communism in 1989 liberalism has been seen to offer protection from the intrusiveness of states and to provide a sanctuary within civil society for those fleeing from centralization. But other East Europeans see it as holding out the delectable fruits of a market-driven prosperity that their societies had been denied by their past ideological and political systems. Liberalism is also the target of misrecognition and ambivalence. In the United States it is seen as a supporter of big government and human rights, or conversely as the enfeebling gospel of the nanny-state. In some highly religious societies, liberalism is tantamount to heresy, falsely deeming human beings, not God, as the measure of all things, elevating the secular hubris of individual preferences above the divine will.

All this is hardly surprising, for a doctrine with such a high profile is bound to attract heavy criticism and suspicion in the course of its history. There are those who condemn liberalism as an officious, hazardous, and enervating doctrine under whose banner both social and personal harm have been inflicted. Many poststructuralists have accused liberals of fostering false ideals of harmony and cooperation, and of being damagingly individualist. Some of its cultural opponents fault it for setting itself up over accumulated and traditional social wisdom. It has been denounced as a manifesto for capitalism, however caring. It has been repudiated as a Western cluster of ideas that seeks to replace or subjugate other culturally significant understandings of social life, offering a cover not merely for large-scale exploitation inside Europe but—no less perturbingly—for the former colonial policies in Europe's ex-colonies. It has been castigated as a doctrine that has failed to give women their proper social due; derided as an exaggerated view of the rationality of human conduct at the expense of both emotion and passion; or disparaged as a rosy-eyed theory of artificial consensus that papers over the vitalizing diversities and discontinuities among human beings.

In sum, liberalism has been adopted by truth-seekers, endorsed by humanists, campaigned for by reformers, cast aside by rival ideologies, deliberately misappropriated by those who wish to disguise their real political intentions, and attacked by those who regard it as a self-deluding smoke screen for anti-social conduct. In its multiple guises, liberalism has been, at the same time, something to be proud of and something to censure and bemoan. Yet, when all is said and done, liberalism is one of the most central and pervasive political theories and ideologies. Its history carries a crucial heritage of civilized thinking, of political practice, and of philosophical-ethical creativity. In the course of its emergence its diverse currents have borne some of the most important achievements of the human spirit. Without liberalism one could not conceive of the modern state. The state liberals had in mind was one that places the good of individuals before that of rulers; that recognizes both the limits and the possibilities of government; that enables the market exchanges that are necessary to proper standards of living; that justifies the holding of private property beneficial to individual prosperity; that releases individuals from burdensome hindrances to their freedom and flourishing; and that respects the law and constitutional arrangements. Without liberal conceptions of human dignity, it would be difficult to imagine, let alone sustain, personal originality and uniqueness. But liberalism has achieved more than that. In its more recent history it has also upheld the concern for the plight and welfare of others, and it has insisted on sensitivity to social differences within societies.

The sounds of liberalism: an initial sampling

Let's listen to some liberal voices over the past two centuries, since it became a recognizable set of political principles, as well as a powerful ideology. First there are the enthusiastic voices:

> Liberalism... begins with the recognition that men, do what they will, are free; that a man's acts are his own, spring from his own personality, and cannot be coerced. (R.G. Collingwood)

> Liberals regard as sacred the right of everyone, however humble, odd, or inarticulate, to criticize the government. (Leo Strauss)
>
> The word liberal is a word primarily of political import, but its political meaning defines itself by the quality of life it envisages, by the sentiments it desires to affirm. (Lionel Trilling)
>
> Liberalism is an all-penetrating element of the life-structure of the modern world... Liberalism is the belief that society can safely be founded on this self-directing power of personality, that it is only on this foundation that a true community can be built. (L.T. Hobhouse)

Then there are the critical voices. In one version, liberals are class-based exploiters of the advantages of the market. 'The practice of this energetic bourgeois liberalism', wrote Karl Marx and Friedrich Engels, referring to French and German middle class interests around the time of the French Revolution, 'showed itself... in shameless bourgeois profit-making'. In another version, liberals transform politics into an arena of disruptive competition and discord, instead of a search for solidarity and unity. Thus the post-Marxist philosopher Chantal Mouffe wrote that 'Liberalism simply transposes into the public realm the diversity of interests already existing in society and reduces the political moment to the process of negotiation among interests.' Many American conservatives employ liberalism as a pejorative term, and relate it to an over-interventionist and heavily spending government, or to an exaggerated concern with the rights of minorities and the marginalized at the expense of responsible citizens, who should not have to carry the burden of other people's failings. The American conservative writer, Russell Kirk, complained that 'the present-day liberal, become an advocate of the tyranny of the state in every field, offers as an apology his intention of freeing the people'.

Finally we have the voices of professional political theorists and philosophers. It is within this group that liberalism is predominantly regarded as a theory of justice and public virtue. As the philosopher John Rawls expressed it: 'The content of a liberal political conception of justice has three main elements: a list of equal basic rights and liberties, a priority for those freedoms, and an assurance that all members of society have adequate all-purpose means to make use of these rights and liberties.' Another version is that of the scholar of jurisprudence Ronald Dworkin, who from a legal-moral perspective defined liberalism as consisting of a particular theory of equality, whereby citizens are treated as equal by insisting 'that government must be neutral on what might be called the question of the good life'. The assumption here is that an individual is the best choice exerciser for her or his own life and that governments should steer clear of dictating moral options in the private sphere.

Liberalism as history, ideology, and philosophy

There are three ways of handling the variety of encounters with liberalism. We could do what many have done and still do: plump for one of the characterizations of liberalism as correct while dismissing the others without much ado as false or mistaken. Whatever we think of such a truth-seeking perspective, it does not allow for flexibility or pluralism in approaching liberalism. Instead, we could try to identify the most typical, or most common, of the liberal variants and appoint it as the benchmark for what is meant by liberalism. We then run the risk that its supporters might misrecognize what they believe liberalism is, and we might sacrifice the subtlety and quality of which liberal ideas are capable by subjecting it to the changing views of majorities. Alternatively, we could offer a map on which to place, locate, and trace the features of different liberalisms, both shared and distinct. Such a map might enable us to comprehend how various liberalisms are cobbled together. With this map in hand, we could assess the contributions and shortcomings of key liberal variants while appreciating the range and power of liberalism as a whole. That will be the method advanced here. The following chapters will analyse the selective preferences people display in their accounts of liberalism, without necessarily endorsing any of them. But, as will be noted in Chapter 7, we also need to be alert to the eventuality that liberal positions are often misappropriated.

Liberals have always seen themselves as part of a tradition of thinking about the relationship between individual and society, and they can claim an impressive pedigree in advocates of natural rights and tolerance such as John Locke (1632–1704) and champions of liberty such as John Stuart Mill (1806–73). Consequently, one well-established method of investigating liberalism approaches it as a historical story about how individuals and societies progress. 'Progress' is the operative word here, as the underlying assumption is that the liberal project entails the continuous improvement and refinement of the human condition, in the course of a gradual and steady process. But whereas liberals have their own unequivocal narratives about the path travelled by liberalism, scholars of liberalism may give rival and rather different accounts of what they think happened on that journey. They may disagree sharply over what the main liberal ideas and the key liberal innovations are. They may differ on whether liberalism peaked in a particular era or not; whether it has weakened as a viable theory or become increasingly resourceful; whether it has betrayed its roots or has strengthened them. Liberalism has changed unevenly in the course of its history. It has accrued various layers of argument over time that have loosely added to its characteristics. Anticipating the discussion in Chapter 3, we can provisionally suggest that liberalism has consisted historically of five temporal layers (see Box 1).

Some of those layers have also disappeared or been overshadowed in several cases. At any point a different layer may be ascendant or in decline and, as a consequence, remarkably diverse conclusions can be reached concerning how liberalism has navigated among them.

Box 1 The temporal layers of liberalism

1. A theory of restrained power aimed at protecting individual rights and securing the space in which people can live without governmental oppression
2. A theory of economic interactions and free markets enabling individuals to benefit from the mutual exchange of goods.
3. A theory of human progress over time intended to enable individuals to develop their potential and capacities as long as they do not harm others.
4. A theory of mutual interdependence and state-regulated welfare that is necessary for individuals to achieve both liberty and flourishing.
5. A theory that recognizes the diversity of group life-styles and beliefs and aims for a plural and tolerant society.

But liberalism, as already mentioned, is also an ideology competing over space in a crowded ideological world. That means that it displays all the characteristics ideologies have in common, as an action-oriented set of ideas, beliefs, and values that exhibit a recurring pattern. Ideologies aim to justify, contest, or change the social and political arrangements of a political community. Liberalism, too, campaigns to control public policy and political language in that manner, but it is of course only one ideology among many, and it has had, and still needs, to struggle for recognition and influence.

On a third dimension, liberalism constitutes a philosophical view of the world, attempting to establish the principles of the good life that all reasonable human beings ought to adopt. In that sense it positions itself above the political fray, setting out the true and unified ethical standards that civilized societies everywhere should, upon reflection, maintain. Such philosophical viewpoints only occasionally take into account the actual temporal and cultural constraints that render the realization of those ideals very problematic. Nonetheless, the elaboration of liberal philosophical principles has been at the heart of recent political philosophy, and we will accordingly devote space to exploring those arguments in Chapter 6.

If, however, there are many liberalisms, they may best be identified through historical and ideological analysis rather than through the philosophical postulation of an ideal-type, which is by its very nature unitary. The diversity of those liberalisms exists on two levels. The first, as already illustrated, pertains to the level of geographical and cultural differences. Even the most universal of liberalisms, were there indeed such a thing, would have to pass through the cultural filters of the society in question. As with cooking, local and regional ingredients and flavours have a considerable impact on the liberal cuisine. In commercial and financial centres, the entrepreneurial attributes that liberalism encourages come to the fore. In societies that have undergone secularization, the belief in human decency rather than God-willed natural rights underpins the liberal sensitivity to, and respect for, others. In societies that are multi-cultural, the constitutional rights to a measure of self-determination of various groups within that society—ethnic, geographic, religious, or gender-based—are prominent in liberal discourse. All those nuances emerge as a consequence of our awareness of where we stand in relation to time and space.

The morphology of liberalism

The study of ideologies also alerts us to another kind of multiplicity. Ideologies, liberalism included, clump ideas together in certain combinations that have a unique profile, a distinct morphological pattern. They arrange political concepts such as liberty, justice, equality, or rights in clusters. The clusters at the liberal core will be those that appear in all the known versions of liberalism and without which it would be unrecognizable. Anticipating the discussion in Chapter 4, we can arrive at a provisional statement based on the analysis of what liberals have actually said and written (see Box 2).

Those seven core elements are the nucleus around which all liberalisms revolve. However, the differences among liberalisms then begin to make themselves felt. First, the proportionate weight accorded to each of these concepts within the family of liberalisms may differ. For instance, some liberalisms might recognize the role of emotion and slightly demote rationality; others might play down the innate sociability of people; others again might prefer a strong form of individuality over a pronounced concern for the general interest. The basic ingredients of the liberal cocktail may be similar, but the quantity of each ingredient may change.

Second, every one of those concepts carries more than one meaning. To give an example, liberty could refer to the absence of external constraints that permits self-determination. But it could also relate to the possibility of cultivating one's personal potential in order to facilitate self-development. It could further signify the emancipation of a group or nation due to the combined efforts of their members to rid themselves of external control, or a free-for-all among unrestrained individuals that results in anarchy or social chaos. Because all political concepts have many conceptions, there is endless contestation over which is the most appropriate to a given set of circumstances. One of the key roles that ideologies perform is to decide which conception to endorse within each of the

Box 2 The conceptual morphology of liberalism

Liberalism is an ideology that contains seven political concepts that interact at its core: liberty, rationality, individuality, progress, sociability, the general interest, and limited and accountable power.

concepts they contain. In other words, they decontest the essential contestability of those concepts by conferring a certainty on one of those meanings, however questionable and illusory it might be. Different cultures across the globe will rule some meanings in and others out. Nor is the choice of one meaning necessarily due to deliberate deception. It may be sincerely held or unconsciously assumed. Ultimately there is no correct formula, no totally objective view, from which to ascertain once and for all what exactly liberalism ought to incorporate and signify. Yet in living our lives we need to create certainties, however fleeting or erroneous, because without them we cannot make sense of the world or reach decisions when confronted with conflicting choices. Liberalism supplies one of the numerous maps available as people attempt to navigate through their social and political environments, and it is a map that has guided many individuals, governments, and societies. We will re-examine this conceptual approach to liberalism in Chapter 4.

Liberal institutions

Liberalism is evidently also associated with political movements, organizations, and parties. Most countries that practise forms of liberal democracy, in Europe or elsewhere, have a liberal party either in name or in programme. Many institutions, not least on the international stage, have seen themselves as purveyors of liberal ideas in the general sense. The United Nations Charter of 1945 emphasizes the pursuit of peace, justice, equal rights, and non-discrimination—principles straight out of the liberal lexicon (Figure 2). But here a gap opens up between the ideological and institutional manifestations of liberalism. Liberal ideologies are generally speaking broader than the parties and groupings that operate under that name. J.M. Keynes memorably wrote, 'Possibly the Liberal Party cannot serve the State in any better way than by supplying Conservative Governments with Cabinets, and Labour Governments with ideas.' But *pace* Keynes, the Liberal party in Britain, or the Liberal Democrats as they are now called, have fed

2. Signing the United Nations Charter at a ceremony held in San Francisco on 26 June 1945.

off wider ranging liberal thinking over the years and political parties are rarely a source of ideological innovation. Indeed, some parties flaunting the label 'liberal' are far from liberal, an example being the Liberal Democratic party in Japan, which is a centre-right conservative party. Liberal thinkers and ideas generally emerge from debates among intellectuals, from the campaigning zeal of social reformers and journalists—including newspapers aligned with liberal causes—and from dedicated pressure groups and, more recently, think tanks and blogs. But due to their public profile, political parties are often taken by public opinion to be the representatives of the ideologies they reference. During the 19th century, Liberal parties were in their heyday and their influence over the ideological agenda was at its highest, though that power has since declined. Parties are therefore only a partially reliable indicator of the ideologies they claim to stand for. They also only seldom contain liberal philosophers working at a specialized and abstract level of articulation, precisely because parties have to engage in the kind of communicable and simplifying discourse that can attract large numbers of voters. Occasionally political philosophers such as Mill have become members of parliament, but in that capacity their influence has not been notable. In the following chapters we will mention institutionalized liberalism only occasionally. It is an absorbing subject on its own, but it will not lead us to liberalism's heart.

Beyond the specifically political hues of liberalism, it has exercised a broader influence on thinking about, and in, the world. It would be no exaggeration to claim that the cultural features of political modernity—openness, reflectiveness, critical distance, scepticism, and experimentation—have taken their inspiration from a liberal mindset. An ideology's impact cannot be measured solely on a narrow political platform.

Chapter 2
The liberal narrative

There is something very unusual regarding the way the history of political thought is usually written about and taught. It is presented as the accumulated thinking of some fifty individuals, give or take. The express route begins around Plato and Aristotle, moving through St. Augustine and Thomas Aquinas, stopping at Machiavelli and then on to Hobbes, Locke, and Rousseau. From there it branches to Hegel, Marx, and Mill, and after that offers a series of lesser tracks into the 20th century. Occasionally there are smaller halts on the way that vary from journey to journey. We will not ignore that tradition, and Chapter 5 is devoted to assessing some of its central liberal players. Indeed, at times strenuous efforts are made to broaden that canon, as in the Cambridge University Press blue books series, so we now have perhaps a hundred or so individuals who have to be taken into account. But think about the following for a moment: could any other branch of history get away with a narrative encompassing so few people, whether fifty or a hundred? Could social or cultural historians pull that off, for example? The reason for the strange historical sweep—or lack of it—of the study of political thought is complex. For one, it was not designed by historians but in the main by scholar-philosophers whose prime interest was in the unique, the outstanding, and the visionary. Second, it was rooted in now-disputed theories of evolution and progress that regarded political thinking as unfolding in a clear sequence. Third, it became a self-perpetuating convention, encouraged in universities, of addressing political ideas as reified and constituting the challenging heart of dignified culture, albeit with a striking Western bias.

Liberals of course colluded in that feat of human imagination, selective and elitist as it was. As suggested in Chapter 1, one way of approaching liberalism is to see it as a story about how individuals and societies change for the better over time. The tale liberals want to tell is about the growth of civilization and the progress of humanity. According to that optimistic narrative, human beings are increasingly driven by a love of freedom and opposition to tyranny and oppression. The cultivation of one's individuality, and a respect for the individuality of others, are held to be the hallmarks of a decent society. Consequently liberals wish to manage the relationships between individuals, states, and societies by endowing people with sets of rights intended to protect and enhance their liberty and individuality.

The prehistory of liberalism

Where does the liberal story begin? The history of the word 'liberalism' and its usages is more recent than the ancestry of many of the ideas from which liberalism has drawn and subsequently embraced. The use of the word 'liberal' in a political sense dates from Spain in the second decade of the 19th century. In Britain that political sense can be found a few years later in the 1820s, as the word began to mean more than 'generous' or 'ample' and assumed the connotations of 'radical', 'progressive', or 'reformist'. But the antecedents of liberalism are much older. We can find proto-liberalisms, or segments of what was to mature into a full liberal credo, from the end of the Middle Ages onwards.

Liberalism began, broadly speaking, as a movement to release people from the social and political shackles that constrained and frequently exploited them. Tyrannical monarchs, feudal hierarchies and privileges, and heavy-handed religious practices combined to create a sense of oppressiveness that became increasingly difficult to bear, and that steadily fell out of step with the advent of the modern world. The rise of liberal ideas is therefore linked to great social changes that were occurring across Europe. One of them was the challenge to religious monopolies, as secular powers sought to escape the control of the Church. It was followed by objections to the uniformity of religious belief and practice from within the domain of religion itself, typically during the Protestant Reformation. More generally, the right to resist tyranny was becoming an increasingly vocal demand, and it culminated in the celebrated insistence of John Locke on the right of the people to dismiss those rulers who heaped on their subjects 'a train of abuses'. But the implied consent was still embryonic. It was not broadly democratic in nature except in the setting up of a political society—a fairly rare event. It centred on the voicing of dissent, not consent. The right of the people to say 'no' to bad government preceded by a considerable margin their right to say 'yes': to fashion desired political practice by mandating governments to act. And Locke recognized tacit 'consent' as a sufficient indication of the legitimacy of a government: silence was over-optimistically interpreted as political consent merely through a person using public goods such as a highway, or renting property in a government's domain.

No less significant was the assertion of Locke and other 17th century thinkers that human beings were born with natural rights. Both of those concepts—'natural' and 'rights'—were decisive to the future path of liberalism. For human beings now began to be valued as separate individuals, seen to possess innate attributes—in particular the capacity for life, liberty, and the creation and ownership of property—whose removal would profoundly dehumanize them. Enshrining those capacities through rights carried a vital message. It signalled the priority of those three attributes over other human features, for they were deemed to precede the formation of societies. It entitled people, once societies came into being, to special protection in the form of a contract between government and governed. Finally, attaching the qualifier 'natural' to that of rights implied that they were not a gift at the behest of rulers, or a precarious agreement between privileged individuals, or a convention that was kept up simply for tradition's sake and was stuck in a rut. Rather, natural rights were simply *there* as an absolutely essential element of the human condition: people were born with rights in the same way that they were born with noses. The theory of natural rights eventually underwent some modification—the American Declaration of Independence notably substitutes the pursuit of happiness for the right to property—but it lasted as an anchoring point of liberal discourse until well into the 19th century, as a powerful statement that established limits to interference in individual lives. By the end of that century, although rights discourse remained central to liberal languages, most liberals no longer thought of rights as independent of their social origins and of social recognition. If the term 'natural' continued to be used, it was mainly by philosophers who employed it as synonymous with 'self-evident' or 'intuitive'—concepts that in their turn possess the rhetorical power to remove something from dispute, as had previously been the case with the term 'natural'.

From another perspective, consider the advice given to Italian princes by Niccolò Machiavelli (1469–1527) on how to pursue political success ruthlessly and efficiently, advice that was judged to be subversive of the ethical tenets preached by the Church. No liberal himself, Machiavelli has been seen by the liberal political philosopher Isaiah Berlin (see Chapter 6) as promoting a world in which different value-systems could live side by side, through his postulation of a rival political code of conduct alongside a religious one. That, argued Berlin, paved one of many paths towards the value-pluralism that liberalism embraces and encouraged the practice of challenging belief systems that claim a monopoly over their hold on the truth. That said, we now regard Machiavelli as a major disseminator and developer of an earlier Roman republicanism. Republicanism offered a popular basis of political power. Its notions of group liberty and of citizenship signalled an affinity with later liberal ideas concerning the self-rule of a people and an end to arbitrary dominance.

Social, economic, and cultural transformations

Another kind of transformation that stimulated the rise of liberalism was the growing urbanization of European societies. The gradual consolidation of a middle class, a bourgeoisie, with commercial interests and property assets, strengthened demands to further and protect the production of, and trading in, goods. The freeing of markets from arbitrary control, or from bureaucratic fetters, was added to the fundamental rights that individuals could claim. Those rights were initially wrested from ruling elites, but they grew to become expectations from the state itself. Rather than just assuming its traditional role of maintaining internal order and external defence, and raising taxes for those purposes, the state was re-invented as the guarantor of a set of rights that also included freedom of trade and respect for property. The latter two were incorporated into what eventually became aspects of liberal thinking and practice. The new economic role of the state was defined through phrases such as 'holding the ring', 'honest broker', or ensuring a 'level playing field'. Economic activities were thus state enabled, not state directed. Voluntary organizations such as banks, firms, and factories, inspired by leaders of industry and other individual entrepreneurs, all located in civil society—the arena of voluntary economic and social interaction—would be the drivers of economic activity and commerce. The state would ensure they had relatively free rein.

As for property, it is a moot point whether its protection and valuing are themselves liberal features or whether the institution of private property is one of the prerequisites to developing fundamental liberal attributes such as freedom and individuality. If the former, a defence of private property would have acknowledged the personal contribution of individuals to their own good and that of society at large through their labour and inventiveness. It would have recognized the importance of justifiable security, incentives, rewards, and—not least—independence in private life in the form of material assets. All those had implications for an orderly and rule-bound public sphere. But it would also have sown the seeds of competitiveness: a virtue for some liberals and a vice—when found in excess—for others. And it would have endorsed the importance of the division of labour, which for many liberals introduced a justifiable inequality based on diverse talents or industriousness. But while critics of liberalism have indicted the division of labour for fomenting gross and unjust inequality, the left-liberal French sociologist Émile Durkheim (1858–1917) regarded it as furthering a beneficial social interdependence, thus illustrating the malleability of liberal ideology.

If, however, private property was seen as a means to other liberal attributes, say self-development, that might explain the fluctuating fortunes of the concept of property in liberal thought and practice—namely, its relative centrality or distance from the liberal core, on which, see Chapter 4. Such variations may have been the outcome of identifying other ways of furthering liberal values, with similar effect. For instance, if income were to be redistributed to those more in need, rather than allowing property to accumulate unreservedly, that might achieve a fairer notion of individuality.

The growth of universities and the thirst for knowledge fuelled by human curiosity were another factor in the planting of liberalism's seeds, harnessing the realms of culture and civilization to a liberal temperament. The search for new boundaries of experience was accompanied by the critical evaluation of knowledge, rather than its passive acceptance. Sensitivity to different forms of human expression, and the cultivation of reflective sensibilities towards what one was studying or arguing, became intertwined with liberal values. In Germany, the 18th and 19th century movement towards culture and education, known as *Bildung*, encapsulated some of those aims. German philosophers such as Johann Gottfried Herder (1744–1803) believed that freedom was attained through education and that the recognition of cultural pluralism fostered individual development. Wilhelm von Humboldt, another German philosopher, advocated continuous individual growth. He was admired by Mill, who introduced his famous treatise *On Liberty* with an approving quotation from von Humboldt, citing the latter's grand, leading principle: 'the absolute and essential importance of human development in its richest diversity'.

Sustaining all that was the enlightenment, a movement of ideas located mainly in the 17th and 18th centuries, which promoted the view that empirical evidence was the basis of rational knowledge and focused on the scientific investigation of human beings in a social context, as well as on its artistic expression. This anthropocentric view of the 'science of man' also allowed for the study of the moral and cultural components of human conduct. It encouraged a non-dogmatic, experimental, and critical assessment of the human condition, releasing philosophical and social thought from traditional restraints. Enlightenment thinkers with direct impact on political thought were notable in particular in France—Charles-Louis de Secondat Montesquieu (1689–1755); in Germany—Immanuel Kant (1724–1804); and in Scotland—David Hume (1711–76) and Adam Smith (1723–90). Instead of religious authoritarianism, they practised an open-ended curiosity, and most of them extolled the ideals of freedom and equality. That provided an impetus to the rational, planned construction of social and political institutions and to the furtherance of toleration. All these were accompanied by a swelling demand that the voice of the people be heard. Initially, that voice was restricted to some of the wealthy, the educated, and the articulate segments of society, particularly through a free and often outspoken press and pamphlet culture. But the idea of broad representation became another building block in the consolidation of liberal principles.

When liberalism met democracy

By the time of the rise of mass politics in the later 19th century the ground had been prepared for the crystallization of liberalism in its political forms. Equipped with those beliefs, liberals were understandably attracted to, and derived strength from, the early 19th century theories of rational progress gleaned from the enlightenment. But their fate was also intertwined with the emergence of a large Liberal party on the British political scene. Aristocratic landowners within the political faction known as the Whigs had been strongly aligned with Parliament, rather than the monarchy, and began to be seen as a force for progress. The moderate political reforms they supported slowly enabled middle class manufacturers and entrepreneurs to enter the political arena. The latter fought for the release of trade and industry from economic fetters and, being innovators, were far more amenable to change than the landed aristocracy. The ideas supported by those commercial and urban powers began to be put into practice. Notable radical reformers such as Richard Cobden (1804–65) and John Bright (1811–89) rose to prominence amongst them, preaching the gospel of free trade and internationalism. The Liberal party came into being as a combination of those groups and became a national party.

One of the chief political impacts of British liberalism was to press for the extension of the franchise through two major Reform Acts, in 1832 and in 1867. Both were cautious steps on the way to democracy, increasing the number of those entitled to vote to male householders. Women, however, had to wait until the early 20th century for the right to vote, agitating for political liberty and equality through the suffragette movement. That right was conceded only following their great contributions to the First

World War effort. The Reform Acts also gradually enfranchised those who had previously been debarred from voting for religious reasons, and the Third Reform Act of 1884–5 redistributed electoral constituencies more fairly and equally, reflecting demographic shifts of population. Another political impact was to pass legislation that reduced controls on economic activity. It resulted in the Liberal party, and liberalism more generally, being associated with free trade and laissez-faire, even though governmental regulation and intervention still continued to a lesser degree and proper laissez-faire was always more mythical than real.

A third political impact was the introduction, from the 1880s, of a specific political programme put to the electorate, rather than just fighting elections on one issue at a time or as a personal contest between two candidates. The Liberal party helped to modernize politics by transforming parties from being exclusively machines for winning votes and putting people into office into ideological disseminators of policies whose role was also to wage battles of ideas. The influence of liberalism as a political theory was immensely assisted by the Liberal party forming governments for extensive periods between the middle of the 19th century and the First World War.

It was only by the mid 19th century that liberalism and democracy began to consolidate what now seems to be an inseparable relationship. Up to that point liberals were wary about what they believed were two dangerous features of democracy. First, democracy could develop into a tyranny of the majority, thus merely replacing the older despotisms of minorities wielded by kings and aristocrats with newer ones. Second, given the abysmal state of education of the population at large, it could perpetuate mediocre rule. That was one reason why liberals were passionate advocates of compulsory education for children: an enlightened democracy required the ability to make good and informed choices. It was only much later—as noted in Chapter 1—that the term 'liberal-democracy' came into circulation, with its message that democracy was not just about winning elections and majoritarian rule, but about how that rule was exercised between elections. Liberals, in turn, learnt to accept that their pursuit of liberty and the discovery of the individual had to operate within the framework of an inclusionary political system, even if it ran the risk of including illiberal voices.

The junction of ideas

The path taken by political liberalism was, however, hardly representative of the broader genres of liberal thought, emphasizing yet again that political parties rarely constitute an ideological vanguard. More dynamic and imaginative versions of political thought were bubbling away, with the result that liberalism began to thrive at the meeting-points of powerful intellectual currents. It emerged as a humanist endeavour, an emancipation of the human spirit, and a force for remarkable social as well as political transformation. A regard for human nature as fundamentally rational, cooperative, engaging in cogent communication, and capable of respecting others as well as showing individual initiative, became integral to liberal ideology. The Swiss-French liberal politician and writer Benjamin Constant (see Chapter 5) identified the 'liberty of the moderns' as the triumph of individuality through the growth of freedom of opinion, expression, and religion, but he also welcomed the participation of individuals in the social body. Thus arose the drive to devising and nourishing social institutions that could reflect and energize that rational cooperation. Initially, theories such as Adam Smith's 'invisible hand' did the necessary work. According to that theory, when individuals pursued their own interests, they concurrently contributed to the good of society as a whole. 'Private gain, public benefit' suggested a natural harmony in the workings of civil society that was sufficient for social stability and prosperity.

Subsequently, it became unclear whether such harmony was automatic or needed to be engineered by human design. That was the problem facing the Philosophic Radicals, another group whose impact on the development of liberalism was considerable. Their leading proponent, the utilitarian Jeremy Bentham (1748–1832), was inspired by a belief in the scientific organization of humankind. The scientific principle he claimed to discover was that individuals were psychologically motivated by a desire to maximize their own pleasure or utility and minimize their pain. But if that was true then the 'invisible hand' doctrine would already be at work and indeed secure what Bentham called 'the greatest happiness of the greatest number.' It transpired, however, that this was not necessarily the case. External circumstances had to be moulded so as to accelerate that process. Consequently the Philosophic Radicals saw the task of social philosophers and reformers as one of radically reshaping constitutions, legal codes, and even prisons, to elicit the optimal well-being of members of a society. Bentham's extreme individualism recognized only separate persons and he did not see society as a unit with its own attributes and ends. The key to his objective therefore lay in modifying individual conduct, while side-stepping appeals to the more elaborate moral visions subsequently voiced by liberals.

The contribution of utilitarianism to liberalism was threefold. First, it emphatically reinforced the view of the individual as the locus of dynamic activity in a society. Second, it advocated the necessity of the planned rational reform of existing social arrangements and insisted that human happiness and well-being were the ultimate aims of such reform. Nonetheless, third, the utilitarians did not seek active state intervention, particularly not in economic affairs. Intervention was enlisted only in order to minimize future interventions, once a society had been set to rights.

But other views were circling around. The German philosopher Georg Wilhelm Friedrich Hegel (1770–1831) contended that basing the well-being of a society merely on a selfish drive, however inevitable to the functioning of markets, fell short of what a state had to strive for. A sense of purpose and solidarity could not be supplied by the extreme individualism of market competition, even if it secured material prosperity. That sense of communal unity could only be provided by the rational state, whose role it was to conciliate the tensions among individual egoistic ends by infusing society with an altruistic ethos. That would be buttressed by a state conforming to the strict rule of law. Only then, asserted Hegel, would a society really be free. The British liberal philosopher T.H. Green (see Chapter 5) extended the ethics of the common good that liberals should seek in social relations and in the state.

Another aspect of the collective perspective that liberalism could contain appeared in certain nationalist doctrines in the 19th century. Nationalism is frequently associated with anti-liberal tendencies. It is often expressed in a strident emotional voice, appearing to prefer the aims of the nation over those of its individual members. In its extreme manifestations it displays aggression towards other nations and ethnic groups, is obsessed with myths about its 'glorious past', and develops leadership cults. But there were also milder, more humane, forms of nationalism that took their cue from liberal beliefs and that were enthused by liberal ideals. Foremost among those ideals was liberty, now transplanted into the increasingly popular doctrine of national self-determination or self-rule. Liberty was seen as a good not only for individuals but for national and ethnic groups eager to acquire the recognized capacity to decide their own fates. Given that many of those groups were under foreign or colonial rule, the plea for liberty became specifically a plea for emancipation from domination by others, with republican or anti-imperialist undertones. Self-determination was thus advanced as a universal and equal right of all nations. The cultivation of national identity was, from a liberal viewpoint, part of the respect due to individuals, for whom such identity mattered. A prominent exponent of liberal nationalism was Giuseppe Mazzini (1805–72), one of the architects of the unification of Italy in the 19th century. Mazzini commended the individual right to well-being but regarded a person's country as the ultimate protector of those rights. For him, a nation was an association of free and equal people bound together by love of country.

The rise of social liberalism

Significantly, liberalism was coming to terms with the fact that groups and communities were formative social units. True, there still were tensions between the more individualistic and the more communal tendencies within liberalism and those were not resolved in the 19th and 20th centuries, nor have they been since. But the flame of sociability, already detectable in the proto-liberalisms of earlier centuries, now began to blaze strongly. The main site of that new illumination was not a liberal nationalism but a liberal communitarianism. A number of factors contributed to that further change of direction of liberal thought.

First, instead of a theory of individual utility as advocated by the Benthamite Philosophic Radicals, a new notion of social utility came to the fore. If individuals could maximize their own well-being, some liberals asked why that could not apply to societies as well. Inspired also by continental philosophers, a number of British liberals argued that society was entitled to pursue social goods, provided that they did not clash with individual rights. Indeed, there were areas of social activity, such as investment in long-term future projects or the protection of marginalized groups, that were beyond the capacity of individuals to facilitate.

Second, new theories of social evolution were gaining ground. The influence of Charles Darwin stretched way beyond the natural sciences. Some theories of social evolution were notorious for apparently suggesting that the survival of the fittest principle operated also among human beings and that—nature being 'red in tooth and claw', in Alfred Tennyson's memorable phrase—competition and the elimination of rivals were inescapable. But another version of evolutionary theory, less dramatic but in the long run more influential, maintained that human beings were becoming more rational and sociable. Unlike all previous forms of life—so the argument ran—that process endowed them with the ability to change the trajectory of evolution itself and to plan the course of their own futures in conjunction with others. Left-leaning liberals were fascinated by that theory's message. It appealed to their belief in human rationality and in the making of valuable choices for humanity at large. It suggested that human progress and improvement were inherent to social life. It also normalized human cooperation as a biological imperative. All those beliefs were now seemingly supported by the kind of scientific evidence liberals of all generations had always sought.

Third, and connected to the cooperative evolutionary principle, thinkers such as L.T. Hobhouse and J.A. Hobson—the two leading intellectuals of what came to be known as the new liberalism—likened a social entity to a living organism. The main effect of that analogy was to emphasize the close interrelationship and interdependence among members of a society, suggesting that they could not survive on their own without the support of others. Why then was that a liberal argument, considering that the energetic and assertive individual had been so central to that ideology? After all, organic theories of society often imply that the whole is more important than individual parts, positing the illiberal message of the sacrifice of individual good for social good. Hobson, in particular, cleverly inverted that implication. A living body was only healthy when every one of its parts was healthy. It was therefore in the joint interest of both individuals and society to cultivate personal flourishing. That form of liberal organicism produced the most striking instance of the combination of the individual and the social tendencies within liberalism and, as we shall see in Chapter 3, had crucial political and institutional consequences for that ideology in the 20th century.

Fourth, liberal reformers evinced a growing sensitivity to the social consequences of the industrial revolution. They began to realize that bestowing political rights, such as the right to vote, to liberty, or to protection from harm, was no longer adequate to safeguard the well-being of a nation. The gradual granting of political rights to the working class had given them a voice which touched the hearts of middle class social reformers. As more and more people moved to the cities, the abject conditions of poverty suffered by the dispossessed could not be justified. Terrible housing conditions, periodical unemployment, sickness, and the lack of education disabled many people from enjoying their newly gained right to representation, which proved to be nominal rather than real. Liberals now argued that political rights had to be supplemented by social rights in order for individuals to achieve full social membership and citizenship. Tellingly, they saw that as an extension of the idea of liberty—liberty not only from tyranny and harm by others, but from avoidable and debilitating deprivation.

Liberalism in America: two instances

In the United States, early 20th century progressivism developed a reformist impetus of its own, though with notable overlaps with British left-liberalism. Its supporters displayed an energetic activism focusing on the removal of municipal corruption and on a deepening of the democracy, efficiency, and accountability of governments. They also backed trust-busting in order to expand the equal opportunities for individuals and reduce concentrations of capital that were hampering the growth of competitive markets. Separately, the intellectual movement around the influential weekly, the *New Republic*—an outlet for progressive liberals such as Herbert Croly (1869–1930), Walter Weyl (1873–1919), and Walter Lippmann (1889–1974)—explored the links between liberty and community, a rare theme in American liberal discourse. Appealing to American conceptions of the 'people' as a whole, Croly developed an organic view of the national interest similar to that of the British new liberals. The philosopher John Dewey, as will be noted in Chapter 5, took some of those ideas forward. However, in Croly's thinking the idea of a nation was allotted a greater role. He wrote: 'American nationality has been created by virtue of the binding attempt to realize certain common political and social purposes... the aspiration for social righteousness or betterment... was thoroughly, comprehensively, and constructively national'.

In Louis Hartz's classic but controversial *The Liberal Tradition in America*, he suggested that the American way of life was fundamentally liberal, an import from the English world of Locke and other European sources. The absence of feudalism had permitted the spread of an American liberalism unchallenged by class antagonisms. As Hartz saw it, 'America created two unusual effects. It prevented socialism from challenging its Liberal Reform in any effective way, and at the same time it enslaved its Liberal Reform to the... dream of American capitalism'. He had little sympathy for the 'welfare liberals', seeing in Croly only a rather agonized supporter of democratic capitalism. Hartz's approach lacked understanding of the range and complexity of the plural ideological beliefs a large society such as the USA would entertain. It took less than ten years after the book's publication for racial and ethnic awareness to explode on to the American liberal scene through the civil rights movement of the 1960s, belying the consensual homogeneity in which 19th and early 20th century liberals preferred to believe.

Applying the brakes

There were of course currents that sought to stem the tides of change in liberal thought and practice. Many of their advocates saw themselves as the true liberals, whether as free market advocates or as libertarians. For the Austrian economist Ludwig von Mises (1881–1973) liberalism was a capitalist theory based on private property. He opposed measures that involved greater material equalization and regarded all governmental interference in conditions of welfare—such as establishing a minimum wage for workers—as authoritarian and contrary to the liberal spirit:

> In England the term 'liberal' is mostly used to signify a program that only in details differs from the totalitarianism of the socialists. In the United States 'liberal' means today a set of ideas and political postulates that in every regard are the opposite of all that liberalism meant to the preceding generations. The American self-styled liberal aims at government omnipotence, is a resolute foe of free enterprise, and advocates all-round planning by the authorities, i.e., socialism.

The economist F.A. Hayek (on whom, more in Chapter 5) regarded even Mill as occupying a transition point from liberalism to a moderate socialism. Hayek considered welfare-state liberalism as liberal only in name, not in substance. State intervention in markets was anathema to many such older style liberals because they believed it undermined the free-wheeling, spontaneous, and self-motivated rationale of liberalism. By contrast, the German economic school of the mid-20th century, the ordoliberals, held that a strong state should guarantee the competitive conditions of the economy by actively establishing a market order and curtailing cartels. Those ideas contributed to the emergence of Germany's post-war social market economy but did not focus on the broader features of liberalism.

On a different dimension again, the flame of radical freedom was nourished by libertarians. Currently a minority tendency that has become detached from more prominent liberal strands, libertarians have insisted for over a century that liberty alone, in its purest form, is the message that should be extracted from the liberal tradition and employed to guide social and political, not only economic, life. There is a reason, therefore, for the adoption of the word 'libertarianism' to distinguish it from liberalism, although it too encompasses many variants. A stress on individualism, assuming the superior rationality of individuals, and on defending liberty of action, voluntary cooperation, and private property, propelled libertarians such as the British philosopher Herbert Spencer (1820–1903) to join in bemoaning whether liberalism had not abandoned its own principles:

> How is it that Liberalism, getting more and more into power, has grown more and more coercive in its legislation? How is it that... Liberalism has to an increasing extent adopted the policy of dictating the actions of citizens, and, by consequence, diminishing the range throughout which their actions remain free? How are we to explain this spreading confusion of thought which has led it, in pursuit of what appears to be public good, to invert the method by which in earlier days it achieved public good?

We have seen in this chapter a convergence of different movements of thought to produce an array of ideas that served to consolidate liberalism. Human beings, rather than nature, God, hierarchical and hereditary rulership, or the weight of history, were now firmly placed at the centre of the social universe. A critical and querying approach to knowledge and learning was aligned with human curiosity and scientific practice, and put at the service of people who wished to control their own destinies. The notion of open-ended reform and development gained purchase in an environment increasingly undergoing rapid change—technological, demographic, social, and political. A growing appreciation of the richness of the human spirit and potential emphasized the importance of valuing others and lent a greater urgency to the reduction of human inequality. It meant the nurturing not only of private, but of public, generosity. Soaring above those ideas was a passionate commitment to liberty in its diverse forms—whether that of individuals, markets, or communities. For liberals, liberty was the engine that made a wholesome society possible, and that could stretch human imagination and experience to their very limits.

Chapter 3
Layers of liberalism

Disconnected and overlapping histories

Liberals and students of liberalism have frequently regarded their cluster of ideas as a unity developing smoothly through time. That view reflects their cardinal belief in a linear progression of humanity towards higher and more civilized ends. But liberalism itself has done no such thing. That evolutionary self-image, wedded to theories of progress and cherished by so many liberals, is not borne out by liberalism's own history. Instead, liberalism has undergone fits and bursts of change resulting both in convergences and separations of its key tenets. That is a consequence of liberal ideas having originated at different times, from diverse sources, and with varying aims in mind.

Accordingly, it is more helpful to approach liberalism as an ideology with complex, interacting layers in a constant state of mutual rearrangement. Crucially, those layers do not constitute a neat sequential chain. They are a composite of accumulated, discarded, and retrieved strata in continuously fluctuating combinations. As will presently be shown, the so-called liberal tradition is a mixture of at least five different historical layers linked, if at all, in ill-fitting and patchy continuities. One reason why the five layers do not add up into a unified whole is because they too often pull in irreconcilable directions. Some do indeed succeed others, but others exist in parallel, and others still disappear and then re-emerge. Liberalism's newer layers often obscure and conceal, as well as expand, the gathered meanings it contains and transmits.

Conceptual historians like to use the phrase 'the simultaneity of the non-simultaneous'—an expression coined by the doyen of that school, Reinhart Koselleck. Applied to liberalism it implies that our current understandings always include new ways of looking at earlier, past understandings of that ideology, as if those understandings live only in the present. Thus, if liberalism once concentrated on non-intervention in individual lives, liberals may now regard the unremitting application of that time-honoured practice both inadequate and occasionally undesirable. Although it still appears in many liberal versions, non-intervention may be accompanied by appeals for measured intervention to mitigate human misery. All those stratified understandings combine to form a rich tapestry of the liberalism we now experience and contemplate.

Inasmuch as no layer can capture the intricacy of liberalism on its own, liberalism cannot be understood without acknowledging their interplay. In the course of those intersections, we may find one major layer (say, the defence of economic markets) thickening and becoming more marked, while another layer (say, the securing of social rights) is present in less noticeable form. But in another instance that interrelationship may be inverted—the previously major theme shrinks, while the minor one exhibits prominence. Indeed, any given version of liberalism may deliberately exclude or debase segments of other layers in the liberal tradition if it deems them incompatible with its own: liberals can be as selective in doctoring their stories as the rest of us!

That constant interplay of layers throws light on the range of existing interpretations of what it means to be a liberal and provides the tools through which to chart the intricacies the term invokes. To do justice to the complexity of liberalism means to attempt to reconstruct a rather messy interrelationship of phases, trends, hiatuses, and sub-plots. An idealized optimal liberalism would include the features of all five layers as they have presented themselves over the past few hundred years. However, that is logically and substantively impossible because some features of liberalism are simply incompatible with others. Accordingly, no actual variant of liberalism exhibits all five layers. All known liberalisms are therefore at most only sub-optimal, 'second-best' approximations of the over-arching ideational resources that liberal ideology can host, and has hosted.

How, then, do the layers interact? Imagine a sheaf of five sheets of paper, one on top of the other, each of which contains different messages liberalism has imparted. The surface of each sheet has a mixture of transparent and semi-opaque holes cut into it, the latter covered with wax paper. That means that through the top sheet you can clearly read some areas of the lower sheets, but other parts of those lower sheets are rendered fuzzy. And of course, where no holes have been cut, the areas underneath are concealed entirely. In addition, liberals are prone to re-arrange the order of the sheets, except for the bottom one, which they leave in place. That early, bottom sheet extols the importance of liberty and rights, and that message can be seen through all the sheets stacked above it. But the view of other inscriptions on the lower sheets will depend on how the cut-outs are positioned on each of the sheets placed higher up. Moreover, as the sequence of the sheets is shuffled from time to time and from place to place, the view through the holes changes continuously. Thus, messages concerning competition may be seen in one arrangement of the layers but veiled in another. Sometimes, too, liberals simply crunch up and throw away one or more of the sheets, leaving a much thinner version of the combined liberal tradition.

Layer one

The first and earliest liberal layer—the bottom sheet—is the most durable of them all. Its origins lie in pre-democratic times, long before the term 'liberal' became prevalent politically and ideologically. The seeds of that liberalism sprouted, as noted in Chapter 2, as an uncoordinated, but strongly felt, 'contra tyranny' movement. It stimulated a restraining doctrine, curbing the rulers' capacity for arbitrary conduct and distancing them from the ruled. That first layer was—and still is—a liberalism of simultaneous release and constraint, one in which spaces are cleared around individuals in order for them to have the freedom to express themselves, to be counted as part of the body politic, and to act without fear or favour. But it is also a restricted freedom, because for any individual to have such freedom acknowledged requires that others be accorded it as well. And because one person's liberty may clash with another's, liberty cannot be unlimited for all. In Locke's *Second Treatise of Government*, he significantly distinguished liberty from licence, liberty being not for 'every Man to do what he lists' but to 'dispose, and order, as he lists, his Person, Actions, Possessions, and his whole Property, within the allowance of those Laws under which he is; and therein not to be subject to the arbitrary Will of another, but freely follow his own'. First layer liberalism is fundamentally constitutional, relating to a *Rechtsstaat*, a state based on the rule of law. In Finland, for instance, this has remained the heart of liberalism; in many other societies, it is only the foundation for the further growth of liberal ideas.

In that first layer, some rights were presented as natural and inalienable human attributes, with which people were born. Nonetheless, they were fragile attributes, often under dire threat, and therefore their safeguarding became the express purpose of establishing governments. The initial association of liberalism with rights, and of the political sphere with serving those rights and thereby preserving essential human liberties, was as a doctrine of limitation both of individuals and of governments, in which the idea of a social contract was preeminent. That limitation was cast in the shape of physical and legal curbs. Special over-riding reasons had to be brought into play for endorsing intervention in a person's space without his or her consent, such as committing a crime or an act of war. It is worth registering those principles, for some later liberal layers partially obscured those messages on that groundsheet.

Layer two

If the first layer emphasized liberalism's role as a vehicle for expressing individual preferences that were not to be interfered with by others, the second layer of liberalism transformed that initial role. Rather than focusing on controlling the relationships between individual and individual, and individual and government, being free now meant being able to interrelate to others actively, with the chief end of self-improvement, material and spiritual. That transformation took the shape of elevating markets to the prime arena of liberalism in practice. 'Keep off my grass' was replaced by 'let's explore new fields'. Markets enabled the exchange of human capacity and epitomized an adventurous sense of open boundaries. A world of free enterprise beckoned, with individuals redefined primarily not as equal natural rights bearers—that area of the first sheet was partly obscured—but as unequal units of energy, endowed with talent and drive, and acting to change their social and economic environments. In Eastern European countries in the later 19th century that was coupled with a call for modernization to catch up with more developed societies.

Freedom of economic intercourse and movement could hardly be formulated as a natural right, for commerce could obviously not be pre-social. Instead, Locke's natural right to property was brought into play. Locke's view was an unusually powerful statement. By regarding property as a birthright rather than the outcome of social or legal consent, he inspired a belief in what the Canadian political theorist C.B. Macpherson termed 'possessive individualism'—the open-ended accumulation of goods by private individuals. During the 19th century, the right to property and to its accumulation was enhanced and reformulated—to a far larger degree than envisaged by Locke—as a necessity for social and national flourishing. A major strand of liberalism thus accentuated the bond between person, property, and wealth.

The second liberal layer held that the unbounded economic and commercial activity of entrepreneurial initiative-takers, manufacturers, and financiers would direct the toil and labour of the newly industrialized working class. Increased production and consumption would stimulate wealth, diffuse knowledge, and endorse the virtues of a self-helping population. Individualism, honest work, and inventiveness would combine, in the words of John Bright, 'to promote the comfort, happiness, and contentment of a nation'. Whether or not all these can describe the actual practices of trade and commerce is beside the point, for the rhetoric of unadulterated economic exchange and expansion became firmly coupled to the liberal doctrine, and also inspired what became known as liberal imperialism. In that particular version, liberals ingeniously intermingled the colonizing of foreign markets with a sense of a 'civilizing' mission and purpose concerning the spread of their wealth-producing, rational, and individualist values across the globe. They also re-invigorated the liberal connotations of contract—previously and famously employed to underpin the formation of a political society as a whole—by assigning it to regulating market exchanges and endowing them with security.

One significant consequence of re-interpreting the state as the guarantor of private initiative and socio-economic intercourse—but otherwise limited to preserving social order and defence—was as a precursor of myths about liberal neutrality: a liberal state and its government should steer clear of offering an opinion on individual choices and life-styles, let alone direct them, as long as the latter were not harmful to others. We shall return to the problem of neutrality in Chapter 6. For now we should note that, even were a neutral state a possibility, this need not entail a weak state. The liberal state of the second layer was expected to protect economic interests vigorously through legislation. In practice it also did so through the power of its army.

For many campaigners, however, free trade had an ethical as well as an economic rationale. Liberal aspirations were vented by Richard Cobden, who saw in the free trade idea 'that which shall act on the moral world as the principle of gravitation in the universe—drawing men together, thrusting aside the antagonism of race, and creed, and language, and uniting us in the bonds of eternal peace.' In sum, the second sheet of liberalism maintained the idea of individual liberty but re-thought the priorities of the state as liberty's guardian. The free will area on the first sheet was re-inscribed, its penchant for limited government now associated with the free trade message that was etched in bold strokes on the second sheet. The task of government was no longer solely to protect against arbitrary oppression but to ensure against obstacles to the smooth running of economic relationships (Figure 3). The second liberal layer marked out a new version of human nature: competitive, potentially aggressive, and insatiable. That such a version could nonetheless bring about 'eternal peace' was a massive feat of self-delusion.

Layer three

The third layer of liberalism involved a conceptual and ideological breakthrough in liberal semantics. Though not inimical to free trade, it switched liberal priorities once again and adumbrated a fork in the road that seemed to detach virtue from intimations of greed. The notions of unlocking human potential and encouraging individual development, of which John Stuart Mill was the most able advocate, would be enabled through freedom of speech and

3. The Free Trade Hall, Manchester, England in the late 19th century. Manchester was a pre-eminent hub of free trade, whose doctrines were often referred to as the 'Manchester School'.

education as the invaluable pathways to beneficial human expression and interaction. While Mill was a powerful advocate of protecting private spaces around individuals, he was equally concerned with what individuals did within those spaces and outside them—an issue that was not obvious in liberalism's first layer. Doing nothing, let alone degenerating, was not an acceptable option—although it could be discouraged only through opprobrium, not force or legislation. Liberalism now took on board the fostering of a maturing and progressing individual whose will was not to be identified at a point *in* time but was exercised through an unfolding continuum of points *over* time. That is the real significance of Mill's crucial phrase 'the free development of individuality': the creation of a social, political, and cultural environment in which liberty would be assigned new substance. Individualism may have been a statement about the fixed uniqueness of persons as separate parts of society;

individuality was the detection of a dynamic process at the core of being human. Temporal development and flow were superimposed on the constitutional stasis of the first layer. Temporality here refers not to the obvious changes over historical time that liberalism exhibits, but to the introduction of the notion of time itself into liberal thought.

We can put that differently. First layer liberalism focused on demarcating a safe area of individual space. It was predominantly a 'let me be and do' liberalism, better known by the French term 'laissez-faire'—reflected also in second layer liberalism. Third layer liberalism focused on the forward-looking enlargement of human capacity: a 'let me grow' liberalism. The rise of that time-oriented but open-ended liberalism, which regarded human growth as a gradual process complementing human autonomy and independence, signalled a new stage in its history. This third sheet concealed those areas of the second sheet that over-emphasized individual competitiveness. Instead, it relocated liberal concerns from commercial exchange relationships to investing in the capacity of people to express themselves. Individual diversity and eccentricity were the prime engines of social progress. But the area of the groundsheet that entrenched constitutional arrangements for securing independent and, broadly speaking, uninterrupted individual activity still shone through.

It needs re-emphasizing, however, that there is no clear-cut chronological sequence between those layers. John Milton, for example, had expressed liberal ideas *avant la lettre* in his *Areopagitica*, the carefully crafted plea against censorship of the press: 'Give me the liberty to know, to utter, and to argue freely according to conscience, above all liberties.' It was not liberty of movement within defined boundaries, or the liberty to follow one's will, that exercised him, but the liberty to give vent to the vigour and liveliness of the human spirit. That absence of limits was an early instance of the third layer, commending not just physical space but the spiritual and intellectual scope for human development.

Layer four

The fourth liberal layer continued the remarkable revolution that was taking place within the liberal family of ideologies. Its prime feature lies in rethinking the spatial relations among people. The individualism of the first layer, including Mill's resolute defence of the inviolability of the private sphere, was appreciably curtailed, appearing semi-opaque. Social space was no longer thought of as separating individuals by constructing protective barriers around them but as interweaving them, and not only on the material dimension of market relationships. That was especially evident in the intellectual and political movement of the late 19th and early 20th centuries known as the new liberalism. The new liberalism emphasized the close interdependence among members of a society, suggesting that they could not survive on their own without assistance from, and support of, others and insisting on that support not as stifling or controlling but as essential to enabling individuality and human liberty themselves.

Second, no less significantly, this layer of liberalism endorsed the earlier liberal goal of protecting people—whether individuals or society as a whole—from undue intervention in their space. But the net was cast far more widely, including the blocking of newly discovered threats to the more limited kind of individual flourishing promoted in layer three. It was now contended that hindrances to human development do not just involve inappropriate physical or legal intervention, or the pressures of public opinion. Major additional barriers existed to the working out of one's human potential, such as the five giants of 'want, disease, ignorance, squalor, and idleness'—in the words of the British mid-20th century liberal reformer William Beveridge (1879–1963)—all of which required eradicating or alleviating. The removal of such barriers did not entail the kind of illiberal positive liberty that imposed a template of self-realization on individuals, 'forcing them to be free'. Rather, it facilitated the liberty to pursue the layer three conception of self-development through positive state action. Hence, third, the democratically monitored state was enlisted to assist in that mammoth task because some important human needs, such as securing a job or health care, were in far too many cases beyond the capacity of individual initiative.

Fourth—a particular feature of the new liberalism—society was conceived of as a harmonizable, unitary entity with shared rational ends. Divisions of class, geography, and even religion were at best irrelevant, at worst pernicious, though practising liberals often fell short of that august view and, as a rule, failed to embrace sweeping gender equality. In Britain, that fourth layer pushed out the boundaries of liberalism in its integration of the individual and the social more than any other European liberalism. Its main achievement during much of the 20th century was in laying the ideological foundations of the welfare state, a thoroughly and indisputably liberal creation. The famous 'Beveridge Report' of 1942, with its plan for post-war reconstruction that would alleviate poverty through social insurance and children's allowances, became a milestone in the rise of the welfare state. In typical liberal fashion it combined private endeavour with public support. The state was transformed into a major, though not sole, agent of public good and public virtue. Similar tendencies could be found in the communitarian and statist liberalism of late 19th century French *solidarisme*.

Last but not least, as discussed in Chapter 2, the most novel aspect of the fourth layer lay in its version of an organic society. The left-liberals a century ago subverted the undemocratic implications of the organic analogy. Hobhouse in particular rejected the conflict version of social Darwinism, holding instead that social evolution displayed an increasing rationality and sociability and set the stage for the emergence of intelligent cooperation. For them, the lesson of the organic analogy was the promotion of individual rights by the benevolent state. An area of individual liberty was conducive both to the individual and to the health of the collective life.

The fourth sheet of paper let in the third sheet's notion of temporality in the form of individual growth and progress but aligned it to the broader compass of social evolution. It acknowledged the individual at the centre of the first sheet but challenged any view of impermeable barriers between person and person, welcoming instead some incursions into private space in the spirit of community, when mutual assistance was the only route to individual well-being. That is why some forms of social insurance—health and unemployment—were made compulsory, to secure a common pool of wealth to help those individuals who faltered under the normal strains of life (Figure 4). The fourth sheet obscured the message of the pre-social naturalness of rights, regarding them as the consequence of social membership—an obligatory gift of society to its crucial building blocks: human beings. Indeed, the salience of liberty in the liberal groundsheet was slightly decentred as it was made to share prime billing with human welfare and flourishing. But liberalism's second sheet—that regarded human relations above all as individual market transactions—was virtually removed from the sheaf by the left-liberals. It took almost half a century for that sheet to be re-inserted in the British liberal tradition, though it continued to be more evident in continental versions. Fourth layer liberals were prone to denounce what they termed 'the Manchester School' with its self-centred economic man, its lack of focus on the underprivileged, and its overlooking of the role that society plays in the creation of wealth. Though they welcomed free trade, it had to be trade emancipated from the control of financial, industrial, and military monopolies. Those monopolies may have grown out of the adulation of unlimited private enterprise but they transmogrified into exploitative imperialism.

Layer five

The fifth layer of liberalism—which is far more contemporary—dispenses with the unitary view of society promoted by layer four.

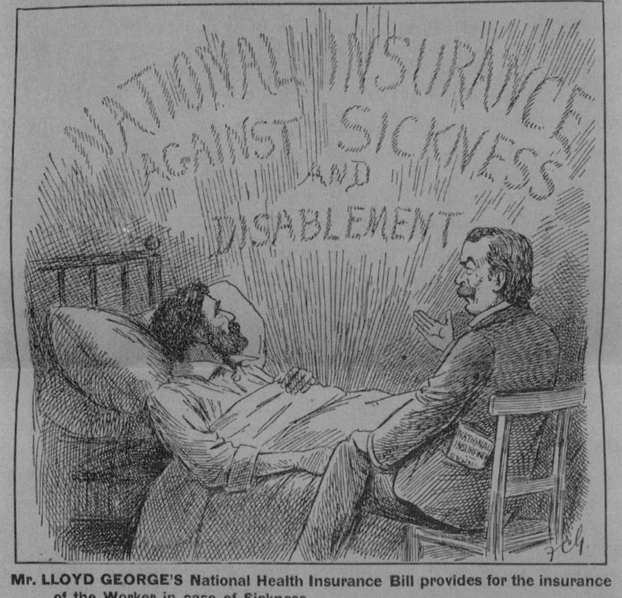

4. The social reforms of the Liberal government in and around 1911 provided limited state health and unemployment insurance and set the basis for the future welfare state.

Sociological transformations and cultural insights have increasingly impinged on liberal thinking. From the early 20th century onwards liberals became aware of the dispersal of power in a society, not as something to be overcome because it set group against group—as in class conflict—but as something to be welcomed. Social and political analysts discovered that society was composed of many disparate interest groups, none of which could monopolize power—a monopoly the state had been assumed to wield by German liberals such as Max Weber. That new kind of spread-out power supplemented and strengthened the legal and constitutional separation of powers. A liberal society had to take on board the interplay not only among individuals, but among such groups, a pluralist perspective that weakened the centralizing role of the state. Liberal politics could be re-conceptualized as a different kind of free market, not an economic one, but one in which a variety of social groups were jostling for positions of influence.

Later in the 20th century, what was known as the 'politics of identity' came to the fore. Just taking account of the plurality of groups competing over the realization of their commercial, financial, or local interests in the public sphere was no longer sufficient for liberals. A more permanent map of human diversity emerged in which the older, problematic categories of race and biology were in part superseded. Alternative categories based on gender, ethnicity, religion, and sexual orientation slowly worked their way into mainstream liberal consciousness, rather than being denied, excluded, or ignored. Liberals in India, for example, prioritize the protection of minorities who are denied fair participation. In the Netherlands the safeguarding of different lifestyles is prioritized over harnessing the state to achieve liberal ends. Those multiple identities—cultural, psychological, and social—are increasingly seen by liberals as normal rather than marginal features of communal life and have been added to the ideational heart of what they profess to hold dear.

Liberal dilemmas

The fifth layer constitutes a difficult terrain for liberals, interspersed as it is with some ethical and ideological quagmires. Its hallmarks are confusion and uncertainty, precisely because it attempts to amalgamate incompatible sections of the other layers. The incorporation of group diversity and uniqueness into the liberal lexicon has introduced a particularistic counter-current that has partly eaten away at liberalism's former—and challengeable—pretensions to universalism. One could, of course, regard the current emphasis on the uniqueness of groups as an expansion of Mill's insistence on the uniqueness of individuals, or at least of some individuals. With Mill, however, that wholly attractive diversity was not intended to revel in cultural diversity but to protect eccentric individuals whose cultivation could enrich social life. Fifth layer liberals are more hesitant. They are aware that, while much social diversity may indeed be celebrated, some has to be eyed warily. Notably, this new layer illustrates the typical, disruptive, and messy features of present-day liberalism, exemplified in liberal perplexity over recent high-profile debates. Those include arguments over female Muslim head coverings (free religious choice or social coercion?); the caricaturing of religious holy men (freedom of speech or respect for fundamental religious sensitivities?); the persistent unequal status of women in many social spheres (gender oppression or deeply engrained cultural codes?); or the introduction of gay marriages (freedom of lifestyles or affront to religious and traditionalist beliefs?). The tensions between such liberal particularisms and liberal universalisms would have seemed unreasonable to pre-1914 new liberals, who professed faith in the harmonious and organic unity of a liberal society.

The markings on the previous sheets thus begin to show dissonance with those on the new top sheet. Individual and group rights were compatible as long as there was only one group—society as a whole, and as long as that society was infused with the idea of harmony between the parts and the whole, as postulated by the fourth layer. But in a society of many groupings, what should happen if one group identity clashes with another? Or if discriminatory practices that liberals considered illiberal, based say on patriarchy or on belief, took place inside those groups? Did the old first layer right to private space extend to groups who would consequently be entitled to do as they pleased inside their own domain? Could liberals tolerate the illiberalism of group practices in their midst solely in the name of diversity and group self-determination? And what would the appropriate reaction be if some groups—for example, some indigenous or aboriginal people—engaged in special demands to have the weight of their voices increased, in view of their past and present invisibility, employing the discourse of victimhood?

Moreover, what if two groups picked and chose different liberal principles from the multilayered tapestry that liberals have woven? What if anti-abortionist pro-lifers push back the right to life to include foetuses at any stage of development? And pro-choicers insist on women's right to decide on what happens inside their bodies, relying on liberty and self-determination—all available in layer one—or on privacy as manifested in layer three (as did the US Supreme Court in *Roe vs. Wade* 1973)? Such indeterminacy and inconclusiveness cut liberalism down to size as its analysts recognize that, like any ideology, its conceptual arrangements cannot offer decisive and permanent solutions to major social and political issues when conflict among them seems intractable.

Liberalism developed as a theory outlining relations between the state and its members. With the increasing blurring of distinctions such as public/private, governmental/non-governmental, civilized/abusive mass electronic discourse, and with the emergence of 'private', segmented, or circumscribed publics who insist on their exclusivity, liberalism faces deep problems concerning its individuality-enabling and harm-forestalling framework assumptions. An ideology whose principles preclude unambiguous answers may reflect the state of knowledge that we have, and even current understandings of reasonableness, but it does not offer the assured conclusiveness that most ideologies fallaciously flaunt, and in which liberalism has joined during its more self-confident phases.

A liberal deficit in democracy?

Although liberalism has displayed its ability to reinvent itself from time to time, the richness and variety of the traditions under the family name 'liberalism' are often compromised. The potential of that richness is still there but its conceptualization and implementation are far from optimal. Large chunks of the first layer were assimilated into the term 'liberal-democracy' but eventually the 'liberal' prefix faded out. Democratic practices are largely thought of as egalitarian, participatory, and inclusive, and they are part of the constitutional equipment of many states. But giving a voice to all people does not necessarily ensure that it is a liberal voice, and we have yet to witness a full-scale revolution that was liberal, from the French through the Bolshevik revolutions, let alone to lesser upheavals such as the various so-called 'Arab Springs'. As Europe democratized in the second half of the 20th century the resounding call was for democratic Europe, not for liberal Europe. Even current appeals to human rights focus on basic first layer rights concerning life, liberty, and dignity, often at the expense of social and cultural rights. The problem is not only the danger that basic rights are mistaken for a fully-fledged liberalism but that in political rhetoric they have come to be disassociated from liberalism altogether. Thus, the grating phrase 'muscular liberalism' is flaunted by conservatives who wish to enforce certain liberties and constitutional practices on some non-'Western' societies but have a truncated interest in the third and fourth layers of liberalism.

Beyond that, the frequent paring down of liberalism to basic constitutional practices and rights is not entirely surprising. The third layer, with its personalist stress on self-development, has run up against numerous cultural and epistemological perspectives that regard social context as the driving force of human conduct. It has, for instance, become theoretically outmoded among those poststructuralists and post-Marxists who explain social life as embedded in hegemonic discursive practices, that is to say, in the manner in which dominant forms of political and social language control human thought and conduct. The commitment of liberals to the primacy of individual agency is side-lined in such theories. But more than that—as global views loom large—the aspirations of the third layer are held to be a luxury unattainable for most people on this planet who are bereft of basic rights pertaining to adequate food, shelter, and protection from violence. Hence that layer speaks to very few.

The fourth layer's antiquated and rosy-eyed assumption of benevolent regulation and social harmony disappears under closer scrutiny, as societies display ever-greater fragmentation coupled with the legal surveillance of their members, from speed cameras, to Internet tracking of consumption patterns, to electronic tagging. Theories of benign social evolution have also gone out of fashion, while the costs of bringing welfare and well-being to all have proved astronomical, made further unsustainable by waves of human envy and suspicion and by large-scale disasters, whether avoidable or not. Slenderer instances of those liberal features still exist within the broad confines of humanist liberal ideology, but the 1990s' claim of Francis Fukuyama that liberal democracy has emerged victorious sounds as hollow as George W. Bush's promise over a decade ago to bring 'freedom and democracy to Iraq'. In particular, as will be argued in Chapter 7, the unfortunately named 'neoliberalism' has discarded the third and fourth liberal sheets, and has partly re-written the second liberal sheet of free trade, leaving a heavily thinned-out sheaf that has little bearing on the complexity, diversity, and ethical force of the liberal heritage.

Chapter 4
The morphology of liberalism

The permeable boundaries between ideologies

Any analysis of liberalism would be incomplete without looking at its structure. That will help us to determine how liberalism's durable, as well as its more transient, features can identify it as a member of a distinctive ideological family. In so doing this chapter complements the approach offered in Chapter 3. We can observe the growth, changes, and diseases of a tree over a long period, and we can study its enduring biochemical properties and shape. Both tell us different things about the same plant. By thus doubling our perspective on liberalism we can attain a fuller understanding of what it encompasses.

The morphological approach examines the detailed structure of an ideology in order to ascertain the typical patterns of argumentation it contains. Specifically, it investigates the minutiae, the micro-components, of the ideology in question with an eye to detecting the configurations of the political concepts it employs. All ideologies, liberalism included, appeal to central ideas and concepts they wish to promote or defend, but each ideology orders its ideas and concepts in a different, and distinctly identifiable, pattern. If, as suggested in Chapter 3, the layers of liberalism are disjointed and patchily linked rather than seamlessly continuous, the morphological approach explores which features of liberalism compose a recognizable conceptual profile. It helps to validate the claim that the various liberalisms that can be historically and empirically observed are nonetheless part of a broad liberal family that displays considerable continuity. After all, the label 'liberal' applied to various instances of political thinking suggests a common or overlapping denominator, unless—as will be argued in Chapter 7—liberal features are deliberately misdescribed. If there are common components, all cases of liberal thinking will display them. If they do not display them then, whatever label they may be given, they do not belong to the ideology that has come to be termed 'liberalism'.

We can now elaborate on what was suggested in Chapter 1. The morphological continuity of liberalism takes into account numerous permutations and decontestations within the liberal family. They allow for considerable internal flexibility among liberalisms and consequently for the durability and adaptability of that ideology as a whole. That flexibility is attained through two features that the morphological approach reveals. First, the spatial arrangements that obtain among the concepts assembled in an ideology allow for many combinations and variants. Ideologies arrange their main ideas in close proximity so that they are mutually reinforcing. For example, liberty, progress, and democracy have been closely bound together in liberal thought since the middle of the 19th century, ensuring that it is difficult to argue for the one without the others. At the same time, different variants of the same ideology also create distance between their favoured concepts and other concepts they regard as harmful to the views they wish to promote. Thus in many cases liberals have disassociated economic liberty and human welfare from each other, especially in layer four liberalism and—with contrasting consequences—in rival ideological offshoots such as neoliberalism and libertarianism.

Second, the variable weighting of the ideational components of an ideology elevates the significance of one of its concepts in relation to another. For example, though all liberals heavily emphasize personal choice and liberty as central characteristics of liberalism, one version of liberalism wishes to bestow greater importance on human sociability and mutual responsibility, while another insists that the end-product of liberalism is a legitimate and consensual constitutional order. So while two instances of liberal thinking may contain similar ideas, the order of priority and import of those ideas can be reshuffled.

All that does not overrule the evidence of liberalism's historical diversity and the partial manifestations of different liberalisms, but it offers a key to decoding political discourses. In doing that it becomes easier to allocate the worldviews and the meanings that political debates carry to a distinct ideological grouping. Of course, there are hybrid and truncated instances of such discourses that may straddle the boundaries between liberal and non-liberal patterns. Liberals will share some elements of their thinking with extensive neighbouring ideological families such as conservatism, socialism, or anarchism—though not necessarily the same ones. Both conservatives and liberals value social stability. Socialists share with liberals a commitment to increasing the life chances of the members of a society, but they do not go about it in the same way, often preferring to change radically the divisions between social classes or even to annihilate them, and they have a dim view of excessive private property. The liberal concern for well-being, individual development, and equality of opportunity is not easily distinguishable from a social democratic attachment to those values. Anarchists have a very strong conception of human liberty but they do not share liberals' ideas about constitutional government.

The boundaries between ideologies are not rigid but permeable and it is up to us as students of liberalism to decide on whether the movement of ideas across those boundaries is eroding the difference between any two proximate ideologies, or whether the migration is limited, so that sufficiently clear differences are retained. In most cases it is possible to say of a belief system or a set of political discourses that they either occupy space within the liberal domain or they do not. If one can discern a durable use of the term 'liberal', there is a prima facie case for checking it for continuities, however mindful we should be of allowing leeway for newer variants as well as the discarding of older ones. By analogy, dwellings across our planet contain kitchens of very different kinds, but they are still recognizably kitchens. Kitchens may have changed considerably over the centuries but they still share the common elements of food preparation sites attached to sources of heat and water. Liberalisms, too, share common components even though they have been adapted to greatly changed circumstances and priorities.

The liberal core

What, then, are the liberal commonalities? What are the ideas to be found in all liberalisms, irrespective of their spatial position or their relative weight within each manifestation of liberalism? As suggested in Chapter 1, ideologies are composed of core concepts that have considerable durability. That means, first, that their persistence can be empirically ascertained by examining different instances of a given ideology and, second, that deprived of such a core concept, that ideology would not be recognizable, or mutate into a member of a different family. We can illustrate that with the concept of *liberty*, or *freedom*. Unsurprisingly, liberty is a valued core feature of liberalism that runs through its multiple versions. Unsurprisingly, if we were to remove the idea of liberty from any such version, liberalism would forfeit an absolutely crucial distinguishing element. It is simply unimaginable to entertain, and empirically impossible to find, a variant of liberalism that dispenses with the concept of liberty. But nor is it the case that any ideology that refers to liberty is ipso facto liberal.

Of course, to state that the concept of liberty is indispensable to liberalism is only the beginning of a long story. To announce 'I am free' is an incomplete statement that hangs in the air. All it does is to suggest that I am not being constrained by someone else or something. It immediately draws in a further question: 'by whom?' or 'by what?' Are other people the potential constraint? Do laws constitute a major constraint on individuals? Are there additional constraints that prevent me from being free? Perhaps poverty, so that I don't have the means to realize my choices? Perchance ignorance, so that I cannot make informed choices? Maybe preventable ill-health, which renders me too unwell to act on my free desires? Possibly the lack of meaningful work, so that I cannot exercise my abilities? Or discrimination on grounds of gender, race, religion, or ethnicity, so that I am barred by social prejudice from living a good life? All those, too, act as constraints on my liberty and we have noted them when discussing layer four liberalism.

Because all those meanings of liberty are conceivable interpretations of what liberty means, we have here an instance of an essentially contested concept, namely, a concept for which there will always be more than one plausible meaning. That happens because there is no objective or final way of ranking preferences among values, such as: is it better to be free from discrimination or free from poverty? However, different streams within liberalism do express preference for some or others of those meanings, and policy decisions, all said and done, have to be made. Consequently, one of the functions of all ideologies, liberalism included, is to decontest the concepts they employ—to remove all their major concepts from contest by attempting to assign them a clear meaning. And because the liberal family is extensive, liberty can attract different decontestations in the numerous variants of that family. Broadly speaking, the meaning of liberty will stretch between securing an area of harmless activity, or even passive existence, unimpeded by physical or state initiated intrusions (layer one liberalism) and enabling the exercise of human potential through actively removing any hindrances that could seriously dehumanize human beings (layers three and four). The decision on which of those hindrances deserve to be removed itself reflects continuous changes in the cultural environment of liberalism. Thus, some emotional deprivations are now acknowledged to be as serious as physical violence, or forms of patriarchy are no longer appropriate in a culture of gender equality.

But liberty is not the only concept endowed with core status in liberalism's morphology. It is one of seven core concepts, and we enumerate the others in no particular sequence.

Rationality is a persistent core liberal concept. Liberalism presupposes the capacity of people to make reasonable choices; to reflect on their ends and ways of life; and to behave towards others in a considered, intelligible, and respectful manner. Some philosophers employ the notions of autonomous and purposive agency in identifying what is rational about members of a liberal society. By that they mean the capacity to plan, to anticipate, to seek the optimal options for themselves, to be entrusted to make sensible decisions for themselves, and often also to live harmoniously with their fellow women and men. Derivative from that idea of universally held rationality is an argument for equal rights and opportunities for every person to express that rationality. For many of the early proto-liberals, rationality was God-given or natural, and that contention can still be heard today among philosophers and moralists. Rationality directs human beings towards a good life for themselves, and towards regard for the preferences of others in their own search for the good life.

A very different reading of rationality is the calculated attainment of ends through the most cost-efficient means. It enters liberalism through economic and utilitarian theories that endorse a self-centred and usually competitive maximizing of benefits and advantages. Currently, that is most evident in some neoliberal approaches that flit around the edges of the liberal family. True, liberal theory has now increasingly come to terms with the importance of emotion and of cultural inclinations in our preferences and decisions, and true also that students of ideology recognize that many decisions are unintentional and unplanned. Yet human reason, and rational communication, still serve as liberal lodestars.

Individuality is a third core concept. It is often confused with individualism, which is a view of social structure that prioritizes the role of individuals and regards them as the only unit of society—self-contained and self-sufficient. Individualism rejects approaches that identify groups, or even society as a whole, as distinctive entities. That is not the case with individuality. Individuality sees people as endowed with a qualitative uniqueness. They are regarded as capable of self-expression and flourishing, and they require those attributes in order to realize their full potential. Individuality possesses spiritual and moral elements of character and will that may be nourished by individuals themselves, but it also depends on fostering the educational, economic, cultural, and health environments that provide the necessary opportunities for that nourishment. Liberal social arrangements are thus evaluated in relation to attaining those ends.

Progress is closely associated with individuality, but is a core concept in its own right. It introduces the dynamic of positive movement and development into liberalism. That dynamic is often seen as part of liberalism's enlightening and civilizing mission, and it includes the constant improvement of material technology and increasing standards of living through human inventiveness and effort. Above all, it focuses on an optimistic view of time as unfolding in the direction of social betterment in the broadest sense. The unfolding of liberal time is not predetermined or teleological—that is, it does not inexorably move towards a projected end, as may be the case in some socialist or utopian ideologies. Instead, it is open-ended. Human development is a continuous process that harnesses and reflects the free will of individuals embedded in and secured through the other liberal core concepts. Being neither automatic nor imposed, it is not entirely predictable.

A fifth core concept that runs through liberal discourse is sociability, though its inclusion in this list may surprise some. An initial clue to its importance lies in Locke's proto-liberalism, specifically in his state of nature, which already is governed by two other liberal core concepts, rationality and the dispersal of power among all. But it also includes the duty of men 'to love others than themselves', indicating a strong interdependence of respect and affinity among people from the very beginning. Locke's state of nature is thus pre-political but not pre-social, because of the concern of any one person for the life, property, and health of another. Out of those modest beginnings there then arose over the years within liberalism the notion of beneficial mutual interdependence, whether economic, ethical, emotional, or physical. That notion vindicated the non-solitary condition of human beings and it even made inroads into market versions of liberalism. For that reason if, as some critics of liberalism insist, individualism is interpreted as social atomism—the fundamental separateness of every person from another—that kind of individualism is not part of liberalism's mainstream profile, though we may find it among libertarians.

Sometimes related to sociability, but conceptually distinct, is the concept of the general interest. That sixth core concept conjures up the liberal claim to include all individuals—and groups—in its purview rather than emphasizing class, race, gender, or ethnicity as points of rupture. Liberals thus appear to be impervious to those distinctions as a matter of principle. The critics of liberalism emphatically deny that liberal blindness. They point out ways in which liberals display contentious prejudices, often deluding themselves that they do not. Generally speaking, the idea of community on different levels implies the sharing of some conditions or circumstances that forge a specific identity of its members, an identity that also includes a loose pooling of perspectives, opinions, and ideas. In the liberal case, the default position of the sixth core concept is the desire to appeal to universal human interests as such, to what unites people rather than what divides them, even to some fundamental consensus. That may refer to a sense of decency, to reasonableness, to mutual respect and equality of regard, and to a wish to promote the collective good of individuals. Even among those who interpret liberalism as a market oriented and competitive ideology, there are emphatic references to the general interest. They often subscribe to a version of Bernard Mandeville's famous 'Fable of the Bees', in which he contended that private vices produce public benefits: the pursuit of personal advantage could result in benefits for all. Adam Smith and Hegel, as mentioned in Chapter 2, had suggested that an invisible hand worked to convert the pursuit of self-interest through the division of labour and specialization into outcomes that were in the public interest.

What then, about the fifth layer of liberal pluralism and multiculturalism? Although here liberals recognize the multiplicity of communities within any society, their relationships are not wholly centrifugal. Layer five liberals simply extend the notion of the general interest to endorse the setting up of conditions under which group co-existence is not only possible but valuable. Decency, reasonableness, and mutual respect become even more imperative in societies where those parallel and interrelated communities of religion, ethnicity, and locality cohabit. The assumption here is that their humanity and pursuit of the good encourages interaction and makes it more likely that they form strong attachments to the other core liberal concepts. But as we have seen, intractable problems still obtain for liberals grappling with social pluralism. The former inattentiveness of liberals to minority identities has been attenuated by a conflicted awareness of them.

A seventh core concept is power, but in a specific sense—as limited and accountable. In a deep sense liberals are embarrassed by power: after all, the historic emergence of liberalism was chiefly in response to abuse and oppression by the powerful. In another sense they realize that governments have to be authorized to make binding decisions, and the making and implementation of decisions always involve the exercise of power. Notwithstanding, decisions in a liberal polity are hedged in and circumscribed by checks and balances, by countervailing power, by constitutional rules of justifiable and hence enforceable usages of power, and, not least, by a dispersal of power that renders it less perilous and that draws in a variety of groups into its wielding. That targeted conception of power inches its way towards greater inclusivity and is put at the service of a community, aiming at clearing the paths towards the optimal—if not perfect—realization of the comprehensive package of core liberal values.

Putting flesh on the liberal bones

These core concepts constitute merely the bare bones of the liberal anatomy. For while they are necessary features of the family of liberalisms, they are not sufficient ones. We know that every political concept is host to many conceptions. Liberty can be licence, or the absence of constraints on non-harmful conduct, or the working out of one's own potential, or reflective choice-making, or civil autonomy. But it cannot be all of them simultaneously, because some of those conceptions of liberty are incompatible with others. Consequently, in any particular instance of liberal thinking some meanings (or conceptions) of the concepts are selected and others abandoned. Detailed examination of the morphology of ideologies shows how that decontestation happens.

As core concepts always rotate through the many meanings they can carry, a mechanism is needed to lock one of the meanings into place, however temporarily. Otherwise ideas are blurred and incoherent, and a fix on political reality—incomplete though it is—cannot be achieved. That process of decontestation, as already noted, excludes all the possible meanings a concept may hold, bar one. For example, it plumps for only one of the five meanings of liberty we have just enumerated (though there may occasionally be slight overlaps between some of them). Logically, of course, concepts will continue to have any number of conceptions, but decontestation is a way of assigning particular cultural, moral, political, or utilitarian significance to a concept, without which social and political entropy and paralysis may ensue. Put differently, decontestation simplifies vastly complex issues and provides the streamlining necessary to get to grips with the daunting intricacy of political argument. Decontestation has little to do with securing the 'correct' or 'true' meaning and everything to do with making sense of ideas, ideologies, and discourse, and with enabling decisions to be made.

Decontestation also opens an interesting window on liberalism itself. The multiple meanings that concepts carry mirror the ideational flexibility and adaptability that is one of liberalism's hallmarks and that has secured its longevity. Tweaking and re-adjusting is something that liberal ideologies perform far better than totalitarian ones, the latter often demonstrating sclerotic rigidity that causes them to crack under strain. But there is a flip-side that liberalism does, after all, share with many other ideological families. It, too, has non-negotiable spheres and red lines it will not cross. Liberalism is intolerant of illiberal ideas and practices, such as fundamental breaches of human rights through torture. Opposition to the death penalty is another liberal constant. In other words, liberalism applies strong decontestations to the areas where its core principles are at their most robust. Louis Hartz believed he had found that feature in America: 'Surely, then, it is a remarkable force: this fixed, dogmatic liberalism of a liberal way of life.' He may have been wrong about America but not about the power of liberal convictions.

Liberalism is no exception to the morphological and practical need for determinacy. As with any ideology, assigning ever-greater specific meaning to a concept is chiefly assisted by the adjacent concepts assembled around it. That band of adjacent concepts enriches the connotations of the core concept and also limits it from embracing some possible meanings. Liberals may surround the core concept of liberty with the adjacent concepts of democracy, well-being, and equality understood as equal opportunities. That pattern propels the decoding of the core's meaning in the direction of an accountable welfare state, in which liberty entails the absence of barriers to accessing crucial social goods for each member of a society—a morphological cluster at the heart of layer four liberalism. That decontestation is sometimes labelled the exercise conception of liberty, inasmuch as liberty is not only a state of being uninterfered with, but a state of actively making choices and finding expression for one's capabilities. Freedom is then not just a passive state of being but a dynamic state of doing, employing one's own abilities that are concurrently enabled through the support of others.

Alternatively, liberals may move the concepts of property, security, productivity, and the rule of law to a position immediately adjacent to liberty. When that pattern prevails, liberty will adopt the contours of protecting the market activities of individuals. It will do so through formalizing ownership rights and clearing paths for economic activity, a morphological cluster at the heart of layer two liberalism. Other ways of teasing out certain interpretations of core liberal concepts relate to the manner in which the core concepts interact. Thus, if we combine rationality, sociability, and limited power we associate rationality with the benefits of mutual human interdependence, whether cultural or economic. Moreover, we indicate that rationality could be stultified by the over-reliance on power in a society. The conceptual permutations seem unlimited, but they are not. In fact they generally settle into the kind of layered patterns explored in Chapter 3.

That isn't the end of the story, however. For once we fine-tune the structure of liberalism even further, we alight on a third band of peripheral concepts. Those are normally less durable components of the ideological field of liberalism, but they are vital in linking the more general 'inner' concepts with the concrete political and social worlds that liberals inhabit. Peripheral here indicates two different interfaces. First, the ideas and practices on the periphery of an ideology are less crucial and more marginal in maintaining its headline ideas. Second, an ideology continuously responds to real world contexts that 'encroach' on it and assimilates them into its fluid and mutating discourses.

Take for example the issue of immigration into the UK, an issue that has been at the forefront of public debate for a while. The concept of 'immigration' impinges on liberal thinking, as it does on other ideologies, but it is not as central to liberalism as it is to some recent populist or nationalist groups. Not counting tourists and people in transit, immigration relates to the entry of foreign nationals into the country and can be categorized into refugees, asylum, job, and benefit seekers. The latter two include both those who have a legal entitlement to enter (e.g. members of European Union countries), and illegal migrants. On the whole liberals have traditionally had a tolerant attitude towards migration for two reasons: as part of the freedom of movement they value; and—in certain cases—as a consequence of humanitarian considerations intended to protect individuals from harm in the form of suffering or persecution in their places of origin. Liberals may also set great store by the economic benefits and skills migrants can bring with them, and appreciate the diversity of immigrant cultures and their contributions to the host culture. The peripheral notion of immigration is consequently channelled through the second band of adjacent liberal concepts such as welfare, humanism, pluralism, interdependence, and prosperity, as well as the core concepts of liberty and sociability. However, some liberals may draw the line at types of immigration such as 'benefits tourism', where non-nationals arrive for the sole purpose of making use of the welfare institutions at a society's disposal; or they may wish to limit the entry of individuals who express extreme hostility and threaten violence towards their new host society.

The concreteness of immigration experiences lends colour and context to the more abstract ideas liberalism promotes. It is often through those 'broker' concepts between actual, specific situations and fundamental principles that an ideology begins to make sense and to become politically and socially relevant. Indeed, the core concepts remain vacuous and indeterminate unless they can be attached to lines of association with both adjacent and peripheral ideas. Hence another way of looking at the multiple members of the liberal family is to track the path of each liberal version as it moves from its commonly held but loosely defined core, through slightly more specific adjacent concepts, to the many different peripheries that inhabit and interact with liberalism. And then, of course, we can take the reverse path: from the idea, practice, or event at the periphery of liberalism back through some of its adjacent concepts. Finally, we can gauge their impact on the core, noting how the latter adapts and is re-interpreted in light of being at the receiving end of those selective channels.

Thus, core ideas about liberty and individuality may be diverted into market practices, once adjacent concepts about free exchange, individual initiative, entrepreneurship, and competition are marshalled into position. From there it is another journey towards the periphery of trade agreements between states, or another periphery that relates pay and social status to meritorious work. And a reverse trip from periphery to core may look like this: a medical breakthrough, such as producing a new drug to treat a major disease, might be diverted by some liberals through adjacent concepts such as welfare and public property rights towards reinforcing the core concepts of the general interest and progress. The result could be a form of socialized medicine, free on delivery and financed by the state. But on an alternative liberal path the medical discovery might be drawn into a different trajectory, through the adjacent concepts of private property rights, or pecuniary rewards for individual inventiveness. It could be routed towards a particular interpretation of the core concept of rationality as efficiency, and towards the core concept of liberty as non-intervention in non-harmful activities (in this case, presumably, the production of a safe drug by a private company, competing in a health market). The morphological permutations are legion and the patterns multiple. But they all recognizably fall within the possibilities that the liberal domain has to offer.

The precise and the fuzzy

The morphological approach does not assume that ideologies have essences, or that their concepts have true meanings. That is a view held by some ideologues, ethicists, and philosophers. It relies instead on empirical evidence culled from many different sources to construct repeated and typical patterns of argumentation that can then be grouped together in an ideological family. Through exploring the recurring patterns of liberal language and discourse, we find liberalism emerging as a complex cluster of internal arrangements. The adaptability that follows in the wake of liberalism's structural flexibility and tolerance is highly advantageous to an ideology engaged in endless competition over its survival in a harsh ideational environment. The permutations of liberalism, however, are filtered through the organizing constraints that the liberal core concepts impose on any of its versions. As with all ideologies, liberalism changes more slowly at its core and faster at its periphery. The former thus appears durable and in focus; the latter sits on shifting sands.

Approaching liberalism as a loose morphological arrangement, albeit one with distinct family resemblances, casts further light on the fragility of liberal boundaries. If liberal concepts are rearranged in different rankings, or if one or two of them are replaced by other concepts, liberalism can mutate into a neighbouring ideology. The boundaries between ideologies are not cast in stone. Ideologies may want to present themselves as unique and clear-cut, but an examination of their morphologies quickly reveals overlaps, shared areas, and mutual permeation. Crucially, it is not the presence or absence of ideas and concepts that differentiates one ideology from another, but the distinct patterns in which such imbricated or common components are assembled.

Another difficulty in analysing the credentials of those aspiring to liberal status is the tendency to inflate one of the core concepts at the expense of others. If liberals run with an attenuated layer two liberalism, emphasizing markets and the power of capitalist entrepreneurship alone but paying little attention to individual development or to autonomous and reflective choice, there is a risk that liberty as freedom to accumulate wealth may occupy too much of the core's space, emaciating the partner core concepts. That may happen, however, when any core concept crowds out others, and the observer has to make a considered judgement on whether what remains in the core possesses a sufficient critical mass to deserve the label 'liberalism'. This issue will be addressed in Chapter 7.

There exist of course other, nominal, standpoints of scholars, according to which we must accept that anyone who professes to be a liberal needs to be taken at face-value. That is not the position adopted by the morphological approach. Were we to accept self-declared nominalisms uncritically we would have, for example, to categorize the Nazis as members of the socialist community because they called themselves national socialists. That would, to put things mildly, stretch any reasonable understanding of interwar fascism beyond plausible limits. That is why self-definition by an individual or group—though unquestionably paramount in any investigation—must be tested against a range of perspectives that emanate from outside those engaged in labelling their own ideational wares.

Whatever we may think of liberal arguments and which among them is better or worse, the morphological approach is there to sketch the map of liberal possibilities, not to voice a view on the value of their contents. Its role is to assist in understanding the actual characteristics of liberal thinking, not to pass judgement. Passing judgement is of course a ubiquitous element of political thinking, and liberal supporters and detractors engage in it constantly. But that is a theme that we shall investigate in later chapters.

Chapter 5
Liberal luminaries

The liberal 'greats'

The story of liberalism, as that of all ideologies, combines social and intellectual fashions and currents with the contributions of remarkable individuals. I have contended that it is a methodological and factual error to condense the range and complexity of liberal history to that of a few people. But it would be equally wrong to ignore the crucial role these 'celebrity' thinkers have played in contributing to liberal discourse and in setting down signposts through which broader publics can acquire access to liberal ideas. Because it is quite common to see the complex liberal semantic field reduced to its 'heroic' figures, that reduction has itself had a profound impact on the understanding and reception of liberalism. It is often not what liberalism has actually been that seems to count, but the way general perceptions of liberalism have impacted on the rhetorical and imaginative power surrounding liberalism through its most salient exponents.

That very specialized liberal intellectual tradition has been largely constructed by philosophers and through university courses and 'classic' historical and literary texts as part of a canon. But it is also the case that proto-liberals such as Locke have been co-opted into a later liberal tradition, when many of their intentions and concerns would not be recognized as liberal. For that reason Locke does not figure in this chapter, even though such co-optations develop their own logic and play an important part in the re-invention of cultural memory. Accordingly, this chapter explores the views of some major thinkers and philosophers who shaped and refined liberal thinking since the early 19th century, when liberalism emerged as a distinct ideology. Some of their theories began as philosophical exercises in formulating ideal-type liberalisms. However, unlike much recent philosophical liberalism—to be discussed in Chapter 6—they became part of liberalism's historical and empirical trajectories. That was due in no small measure to the way these thinkers engaged extensively with the political issues of their day.

We begin with four British thinkers who between them illustrate a markedly consistent thread in the development of liberal thought, combining aspects of layer one with layers three and four—a thread that was taken up by other liberals, and unravelled by others still. This emphasis can be justified by a common denominator that notably changed the course of liberalism by opening up the broader potential of its ideas. Some would argue that since then alternative versions of liberalism are mostly rearguard and defensive moves, purist attempts to distil an unsullied or 'authentic' liberal essence, if not outright usurpations of the label. On the other hand, those alternative versions often decry the proponents of layers three and four as betrayers, or at least distorters, of what *they* regard as liberalism—Hayek, as we shall see, is one such instance.

John Stuart Mill (1806–73)

In the pantheon of secular liberal saints, the place of John Stuart Mill is assured. Whenever liberal ideas are discussed, sooner or later Mill becomes a major, if not the major, point of reference. Mill, let it be said immediately, was not typical of liberal thinking. If typical implies normal, Mill was exceptional in his acuteness, powers of imagination, dexterity of analysis, and breadth of comprehension. If we seek the normal liberal thinking of the 19th century, we need to look at pamphlets, newspapers, Parliamentary debates, and other conventional writers. If we want liberal thought at its best, Mill is a suitable starting point. He merits investigation both as a producer of complex philosophical arguments and as a disseminator of ideas to a general public that propelled liberal ideology in new directions. If political parties are ideological stragglers, philosophers of Mill's ilk are ideological trail-blazers. Mill may not be entirely representative of his times, but he was instrumental in giving liberalism a powerful and influential voice well beyond the borders of the United Kingdom.

Mill's elucidations of liberal thought are manifold. In his famous essay 'On Liberty', published in 1859, he stipulated a divide between self-regarding and other-regarding actions, a distinction that highlighted the boundary between the public and private spheres that became one of liberalism's hallmarks. Self-regarding actions were those with which no one had a right to interfere. Among those, Mill listed decisions about one's personal safety, one's tastes and beliefs, and the purchase of drugs and medicines as long as they were clearly labelled. In all those cases, individual reason was to be relied on and, even if people made mistaken decisions, it was always better that they learn from these than that they be directed by others. Other-regarding actions were far more common, given that most individual actions affect others. But they too could be engaged in freely by individuals unless they would cause injury. That rule was known as the harm principle and found in far earlier accounts of natural law and duties, including Locke's. Mill, however, elaborated on it markedly. Mere inconvenience to others, or offence, were insufficient causes for intervention in an individual's actions. Intervention was justified only when other-regarding actions were critically detrimental to the interests of other members of a society. Mill's notion of harm to others was narrow by today's standards. It comprised physical damage and legal compulsion, or the undue pressure of public opinion, but not psychological, emotional, or historical harms of oppression. In the 19th century the conceptual apparatus for identifying such additional harms as equally dehumanizing was barely available. Still, the harm principle and the integrity of individual space have remained distinguishing features of modern liberalism. And Mill's commitment to the freedoms of thought, speech, and association as the indicators of a decent, open society, without which neither individual nor society could thrive, remained paramount.

That was not Mill's only, or even main, contribution to liberalism. He was one of the first to transform utilitarianism from a pleasure-seeking theory into a more refined doctrine. He replaced the utilitarians' focus on fleeting pleasures with a solid insistence on the permanent interests of people, concentrating on their self-development and insisting that they were progressive beings. That idea of improvement had previously not been prevalent in utilitarianism, as its precept of maximizing one's pleasure did not have to involve any idea of personal growth.

Ultimately, Mill bequeathed to the liberal tradition a more sophisticated understanding of its values. As already noted in Chapter 3, he saw liberalism as based on a triple conceptual combination—even if the title of his essay referred to liberty alone—centred on the 'free development of individuality':

> If it were felt that the free development of individuality is one of the leading essentials of well-being; that it is not only a co-ordinate element with all that is designated by the terms civilisation, instruction, education, culture; but is itself a necessary part and condition of all those things; there would be no danger that liberty should be undervalued...

In this inner circle of liberal concepts, liberty was both enhanced and constrained. It was enhanced because it was purposive, understood as the unfolding of human potential. It was constrained—although not fully—because the licence to do nothing or to disrupt one's capacity to lead a good life was frowned upon. Development was specifically located in an individual's will, emanating from within, not imposed from without. And individuality was a substantive ethical ideal and the route to cultivating character. It conjured up the attributes of vigour, variety, and originality—giving full rein to individual diversity. It entailed designing one's own life-plan. Above all, it involved the exercise of choice, an exercise absolutely essential to judgement, discriminatory feeling, and moral preference.

Thomas Hill Green (1836–82)

The new currents that were beginning to flow through liberalism got an unexpected boost through the often obscure and difficult writings of T.H. Green, a philosophy tutor at Balliol College, who was a prominent member of the British school of Idealism. Many of those who attended his lectures found them abstract and hard to follow, and his prose would certainly not seem an obvious choice through which to disseminate ideological innovation. Yet Green articulated crucially important insights and displayed occasional flashes of rhetorical brilliance, which go to show that the incisive rendering of an idea can be picked up by larger political publics. Idealism, as the name indicates, accorded a fundamental and pre-eminent status to the ideas, values, and obligations that underpinned social life. While Mill recognized the social component of human existence, Green extended the idea of sociability, insisting that individual thought and conduct could not be detached from the community of cooperating fellow individuals in which a person was always located. Indeed, Green contended that if individuals carried out their moral duties while valuing and recognizing others for possessing the same potential, they were at their freest. To be free was none other than to be rational and ethical, to will what was true and good, unencumbered by clouded judgement. For Green that was an eternal truth, reflecting God's will, and it guided people towards their ultimate perfection. For later liberals, that morality could just as successfully be retained in secular form.

Green demonstrates one long-standing tendency in liberal thinking—the assumption that there are independent and immutable standards of good behaviour, both for an individual on his or her own and for the interactions among individuals. Decency, respect, tolerance, and moderation were some of the features of that good conduct. That struck a chord among many thoughtful late-Victorians who had become increasingly uneasy with the harsh and selfish bargains that economic and commercial life appeared to dictate. In a rare foray into popular language, Green explained himself more clearly, delivering in 1881 a famous public lecture called 'Liberal Legislation and Freedom of Contract'. It set the tone for the subsequent belief of left-liberals that personal development and mutual interdependence were complementary rather than contradictory aspects of a common good. Here also lies Green's important contribution to the idea of freedom, which was ultimately reflected in modern welfare state thinking. Rising to the occasion in a spirited rhetorical flourish, Green asserted that freedom was not just being left alone but a positive ability to act, together with others:

> We shall probably all agree that freedom, rightly understood, is the greatest of blessings—that its attainment is the true end of all our effort as citizens. But when we thus speak of freedom, we should consider carefully what we mean by it. We do not mean merely freedom from restraint or compulsion. We do not mean merely freedom to do as we like irrespectively of what it is that we like. We do not mean a freedom that can be enjoyed by one man or one set of men at the cost of a loss of freedom to others. When we speak of freedom as something to be so highly prized, we mean a positive power or capacity of doing or enjoying something worth doing or enjoying, and that, too, something that we do or enjoy in common with others.

We have seen that the precise meaning of liberty, or freedom, as is the case with all political concepts, is essentially contested. As one of the first to suggest a distinction between positive and negative liberty, Green contributed to the fundamental disagreement among liberals as to the implications of liberty. Even in his cautious and considered language, Green was sounding a radical note that challenged existing social arrangements and assessed individual conduct by the personal improvement and the social benefits freedom brought in its wake. The growth of freedom was measured by the greater power of the body of citizens to make 'the most and best of themselves'—a view embodying the tail end of the optimistic enlightenment belief in human perfectibility. But Green's was not the extreme version of positive liberty later excoriated by Isaiah Berlin, one in which the rational self-mastery associated with a higher nature or 'true' self would be taken up by an oppressive social grouping, bent on coercing individuals to conform to its uniform interpretation of what was good for its members. The voices of individuals could not be usurped by a manipulator speaking on their behalf and 'forcing them to be free', in Rousseau's famous phrase.

Leonard Trelawny Hobhouse (1864–1929)

L.T. Hobhouse, together with his colleague J.A. Hobson, was the leading exponent of the new liberalism that changed the focus of liberal thought at the turn of the late 19th–20th centuries. Hobhouse is of special interest to students of liberalism because he had one foot firmly in the philosophical domain and another in the world of quality journalism. Almost uniquely, Hobhouse spoke the two liberal languages of the time: as formulator of a general theory of liberalism and as a constructor of a working and living liberal ideology, moving easily between the two. His most famous book, *Liberalism*, published in 1911, was an inspired reformulation of the liberal ethos, in a popularly written and widely disseminated format. It is still in print more than a century later and is unrivalled as a now classic account of modern left-liberal thinking. In addition to holding the first chair of sociology at the London School of Economics and Political Science, Hobhouse was an editorial writer for the leading liberal newspaper of the time, the *Manchester Guardian*. Through those editorial comments, Hobhouse demonstrated how the general precepts of liberalism could be applied to many concrete and pressing social and political issues. In tandem with Hobson, Hobhouse helped to steer progressive public opinion towards embracing the social liberalism associated with the new liberals.

The idea of harmony among human beings as the natural outcome of social evolution guided much of Hobhouse's theories and was strengthened by his scientific bent of mind—his field studies also entailed lengthy periods of observation at a Manchester zoo. Hobhouse believed that human rationality was active and purposive. He pushed Mill's emphasis on human development further out by asserting optimistically that it encompassed both an increased ethical awareness and a conscious and deliberate interdependence among people. Whereas for Mill development ensured the control of individuals over their lives and the maturing of their characters, Hobhouse claimed that evolutionary development also replaced competition with rational sociability; indeed, human beings were the first product of the evolutionary process that could direct its own evolution. The end-result of social evolution was not only a free individual but a harmonious community, guided by a benevolent, democratic state.

At the heart of Hobhouse's liberal vision was a project of social reform. Society was defaulting on its responsibility towards its members because it failed to pursue the common good. That included optimizing opportunities for individual development and harmonizing potentially conflicting human ends. The community was seen as a producer of social goods, the main good being the well-being of its members. But the consequence of that argument was intriguing: the community was itself a rights-bearer alongside the rights of its individual citizens. Too many needs, although vital for individual flourishing, were beyond individual reach. Hobhouse belonged to a new generation of progressive thinkers who realized that the liberal end of encouraging human growth and expression would be frustrated unless the community possessed the right to help individuals attain their personal potential. Liberty was now irrevocably twinned with social cooperation:

> Mutual aid is not less important than mutual forbearance, the theory of collective action no less fundamental than the theory of personal freedom…the life of the individual…would be something utterly different if he could be separated from society. A great deal of him would not exist at all.

The idea behind that was that each person was both a cherished individual *and* a member of a sustaining social group. Although the divide between public and private still obtained, the social side of individuals was central to their very being, both as givers and as receivers. Hobhouse advocated the public right to work and to a living wage, supported unemployment and health insurance (introduced by the Liberal government in 1911), and was also an early enthusiast for universal old-age pensions. Nonetheless, the state was not there to compete with individual initiative but to facilitate it by redistributing material goods and hence life-chances to those who were disadvantaged through personal misfortune or unfair social arrangements. Only then could a liberal society discharge its fundamental responsibility towards its members.

Hobhouse's view of social harmony and of the convergence of human rationality on shared understandings of the common good was an ethical ideal that underpinned his faith in the overcoming of conflict. The First World War, with its battlefields of unleashed violence and the resurgence of an over-interventionist state, rocked his earlier optimistic convictions but did not change them substantially.

John Atkinson Hobson (1858–1940)

Although less punctilious in his argumentation than the philosophers we have just discussed, J.A. Hobson was the most original and imaginative of the new liberals of his generation. Hobson was an independent writer and a journalist as well as an influential social critic and economist. He made his name by foreshadowing some of Keynes' economic theories, and created a notable public impression as a vociferous critic of British imperialism. Both over-saving and the unequal distribution of wealth, Hobson argued, restricted the overall purchasing power of the British people. The poor ended up with insufficient income to survive in dignity and their consequent under-consumption created economic crises as well as personal misery, while the well-to-do accumulated more than they could spend. Imperialism was partly the result of that maldistribution, as financial capitalists and manufacturers turned to overseas outlets for investing their surplus wealth, furthering economic greed, aggression, and militarism, and exploiting the political control of colonies to those purposes.

Hobson's radicalism, however, was powerfully directed inwards as well as abroad. Through extensive journalistic and lecturing activities, he propagated advanced ideas of social reform, many of which found their way into the ideology and practices of the 20th century British welfare state. As did other liberals, he grappled throughout his life with the balance between the individual and the social nature of human beings. That included the recognition that society too was a maker of values, a producer and a consumer. Hobson subscribed to a more pronounced organic theory of society than that of his colleagues. Venturing beyond the views of his friend Hobhouse, Hobson believed that society had a life and purpose of its own that paralleled those of its members. Yet he was keen to insist that the organic analogy nonetheless reinforced liberal individualism. Only by nourishing the well-being of each individual and securing their opportunities to express themselves through democratic arrangements could the health of the whole be promoted.

Hobson's striking contribution to liberal thinking is most evident in his *The Crisis of Liberalism* (1911), which propounded a vision of liberal welfare more advanced than anything achieved to date, and which endorsed the 'fuller and more positive liberty to which the Liberalism of the future must devote itself.' The liberal state, he believed, should provide all the necessities that people could not procure for themselves, freeing individuals to develop the creative and individualistic artistic aspect of labour. In a memorable statement Hobson wrote:

> Liberalism is now formally committed to a task which certainly involves a new conception of the State in its relation to the individual life and to private enterprise.... From the standpoint which best presents its continuity with earlier Liberalism, it appears as a fuller appreciation and realisation of individual liberty contained in the provision of equal opportunities for self-development. But to this individual standpoint must be joined a just apprehension of the social, viz., the insistence that these claims or rights of self-development be adjusted to the sovereignty of social welfare.

And he elaborated: 'Free land, free travel, free power, free credit, security, justice and education, no man is "free" for the full purposes of civilised life to-day unless he has all those liberties.'

As did his fellow left-liberals, Hobson was at pains to point out that the new liberalism differed significantly from socialism, both because it rejected universal public ownership and because it rebuffed the mechanical, averaging, and centralizing inclinations socialists were thought to advocate. But the modern study of ideologies now denies the existence of stark and impermeable boundaries between ideologies. The forms of liberalism endorsed in Britain a century ago were broadly speaking social-democratic at their heart. That variant of liberal social-democracy was clearly located within the circle of the great liberal family, even if the intense rivalries between political parties tended to obscure such subtle shadings.

In addition to the four British liberal thinkers, a slight step back in time is necessary to recognize the significant contribution of Mary Wollstonecraft (1759–97) to liberalism. Wollstonecraft was a political essayist, writer, educationalist, and moral philosopher, who believed passionately in human rationality, for which liberty and political rights were essential. Her major input into the incipient liberal tradition was through her famous book, *A Vindication of the Rights of Woman*. In that volume she argued that women had to be educated to become rational and independent. That would improve their social roles considerably as good wives and mothers as well as citizens. Advanced as it was for her time, 20th century feminists distanced themselves from that traditional role-assignment and from Wollstonecraft's message for women to emulate men. But Wollstonecraft was a major pioneer of women's rights and of treating women equally:

> Women, I allow, may have different duties to fill, but they are human duties, and the principles that regulate the discharge of them... must be the same. To become respectable, the exercise of their understanding is necessary, there is no other foundation for independence of character.

Wollstonecraft concluded: 'Let woman share the rights, and she will emulate the virtues of man, for she must grow more perfect when emancipated.'

The wider liberal net

Even though Britain was a powerhouse of liberal thought, continental Europe and the USA hosted major varieties of liberalism bearing their own characteristics. We shall briefly look at some representative thinkers. In France Benjamin Constant

(1767–1830), an early employer of the term 'liberal', focused on two main features. The first was a theory about the transformation of the idea of liberty from ancient to modern times, adapting in the process to the complex commercial practices of 19th century society. For Constant that meant a decline in the central authority of a small community and its replacement by what we would now call civil society, independent and socially mobile. Liberalism manifested itself in the increase of personal, autonomous opportunities and choices, and in the prosperous production of material goods for all. But that was not a claim concerning the innate universalism of liberalism to be found among some 20th century liberal philosophers; rather, it was an empirical observation about the historic mutation of liberalism in relation to changing social circumstances.

The second feature was equality before the law, the emphasis being on constitutional representation, peace, and liberty from arbitrary government. Constant combined that with a strong resistance to governmental intervention in economic affairs, as a commercial society would best function under conditions of laissez-faire. The need for representation reflected the impossibility of direct political participation due to the wealth-creating commitments of individuals. Yet, crucially, that wealth-creation released individuals to engage in cultural and spiritual pursuits, retaining the civilizing aspect that liberalism was supposed to enable. Constant explained:

> The aim of the moderns is the enjoyment of security in private pleasures; and they call liberty the guarantees accorded by institutions to those pleasures... Individual liberty, I repeat, is the true modern liberty. Political liberty is its guarantee, consequently political liberty is indispensable. But to ask the peoples of today to sacrifice, like those of the past, the whole of their individual liberty to political liberty, is the surest means of detaching them from the former and, once this result has been achieved, it would be only too easy to deprive them of the latter.

In Germany, towards the end of the 18th century, the philosopher and linguist Wilhelm von Humboldt (1767–1835) published a treatise on the limits of state intervention that, when translated half a century later into English, profoundly influenced Mill. The opening sentence of its second chapter was quoted by Mill in full in his *On Liberty*:

> The true end of Man, or that which is prescribed by the eternal and immutable dictates of reason, and not suggested by vague and transient desires, is the highest and most harmonious development of his powers to a complete and consistent whole.

Freedom and diversity were for Humboldt, as for Mill, the two prerequisites for the full development of the individual. As with many German philosophers of the time, the importance of culture, education, and enlightenment (subsumed under the German term *Bildung*) was regarded as central to a full life. This enabled the cultivation of moral and intellectual powers—all within the framework of spontaneous activity. Above all, Humboldt called for the removal of as many political and legal fetters as were consistent with promoting individual freedom and progress. In one sense it was a theory that spoke more clearly to the British than to the Germans. English political thought, from its early modern stages, had emphasized freedom of individual action until such point as harm to others ensued. German political thought had evolved a deep respect for the role of law—and the rule of law—as directing individual conduct towards accepted rational ends, whether or not within a liberal context. But in another sense, the insistence on achieving a degree of culture that established the appropriate moment for freedom and hence for minimizing state intervention became a keystone of German political thinking.

Max Weber (1864–1920), the eminent German sociologist, presented another side of liberalism. His sociological and historical analyses of the German bourgeoisie, as well as of the state, led him to conclude that in order to protect society from extreme bureaucratization, a class of responsible, committed, and ethical leaders would have to emerge. He argued that the charismatic leader would become the guarantor of individualism, supported partly by a mass democracy searching for the disruption of authoritarian patterns of government. This elitist liberalism picked up a theme rarely acknowledged by liberals themselves. Liberalism was a product of the middle classes, and its values—however desirable to progressives—were often chosen and formulated by cultural minorities: the educated, the politically alert, and the relatively well-to-do. It was of course also a liberalism that respected the rule of law but it was not strongly egalitarian.

Weber's liberalism, as that of his contemporary Friedrich Naumann (1860–1919) was also permeated by a strong nationalism that was muted—though not entirely absent—in other forms of liberalism. True, national self-determination had been a plank of 19th century European liberalism, but both Weber and Naumann went beyond that in their enthusiasm for national power and prosperity. The nation was not a simple object of aggrandisement, however, but the repository of the country's skills, expertise, ethos, and spirit resting, in Weber's words, on 'deeply rooted psychological foundations'. The nation state was the site of a balancing act between the rational state and the often irrational, or arational, 'Volk'. Naumann added another strand to that German path of liberalism: a more social variant. His interest in planning, organization, and the attainment of welfare ends acknowledged the forces of economic modernization and the need for the industrial and technical progress of the community at large. But in prioritizing those over individual ethical development, Naumann was teetering on the edge of the liberal domain and was brought back only by his concern for the development of individual personality.

In Italy, Benedetto Croce (1886–1952) demonstrated a more visionary side to continental liberalism than the one emanating from the concrete historical and sociological preoccupations of German liberals. Croce was a philosopher and occasional politician who had studied Hegel and was influenced by him. He had moved from supporting fascism to advocating liberalism. In his *Politics and Morals*—a collection of essays written largely in the 1920s—Croce subscribed to a grand conception of liberalism that identified it not as a particular political doctrine but as 'a complete idea of the world and of reality.' Unlike most other noted liberal theorists, Croce saw in liberalism the expression of divine wisdom, of a higher morality. But it was also one that rejected the 'mathematical and mechanistic' tendencies of socialism for an equality based on a common humanity. Indeed the unequal ownership and distribution of property was acceptable to liberals as long as it did not suppress an enquiring and critical spirit. Although human beings strove for improvement, they were imperfect and capable of error.

That humanistic version of liberalism countered liberal experimentation and tentativeness with an unchallengeable ethics. Croce thus reflected the kind of dialectic tension displayed by his type of Idealist thought, as well as the uncertainties and fragilities of human conduct that perceptive liberals had come to recognize. Far more than Mill and Hobhouse, with their smoother visions of human evolution, Croce regarded setbacks, struggle, and antagonism as elements of the real world liberalism had to confront and take heed of, and which its spirit would ultimately overcome. Against the backdrop of the rise of Italian fascism and various types of continental authoritarianism, that had become a particularly poignant observation:

> ...the liberal mind regards the withdrawing of liberty and the times of reaction as illnesses and critical stages of growth, as incidents and steps in the eternal life of liberty...the liberal conception is not meant for the timid, the indolent and the pacifist, but wishes to interpret the aspirations and the works of courageous and patient,

of belligerent and generous spirits, anxious for the advancement of mankind and aware of its toils and of its history.

Italian linguistic practice helpfully distinguishes between *liberalismo* and *liberismo*, a distinction central to a famous dispute between Croce and the Italian economist and politician Luigi Einaudi (1874–1961). *Liberalismo* relates to the fully-fledged political and ethical conception of liberalism, while *liberismo* refers to its economic, free-enterprise aspects. Whereas in German, and even more so in French, contexts the tendency—as was Einaudi's—was and still is to conflate the two, Croce sought to separate them out. It is, as we have seen in Chapter 3, debatable whether economic liberalism alone contains sufficient components of the fuller family of liberalisms. As Croce put it succinctly, 'the difficulty appears as soon as we give to the system of free enterprise the value of a norm'. That created conflict with ethical and political liberalism, which had a different set of guiding norms, not based on egoistic and hedonistic considerations of utility.

Carlo Rosselli (1899–1937) was an Italian socialist thinker and activist, ultimately murdered at Mussolini's behest. Adversity and, indeed, oppression were fertile ground for the minority of continental dissidents who had the courage to express their anti-totalitarian views in the face of grave personal risk. That aside, Rosselli commands attention not only because of the substance of his ideas—it could be argued that he was not a major thinker in his own right—but because he illustrates the difficulties we find in categorizing left-liberalism in a comparative perspective. The boundaries between left-liberalism and moderate socialism, or social-democracy, are highly permeable and the space those adjoining ideological positions occupy overlaps considerably. Croce had already paid homage to Hobhouse and to the latter's phrase 'liberal socialism', although 'social liberalism' would have described Hobhouse's position more accurately. Rosselli made his mark with a book called *Liberal Socialism*, published in 1930. He saw the essence of socialism in the moral attraction of liberty and, like Croce, attempted to consolidate an intellectual and political position that was anti-fascist as well as inimical to a state-run economy. Rosselli shared with other social-democrats—such as Eduard Bernstein in Germany—the belief that a moderate socialism was the inheritor, and better utilizer, of liberal values. A political liberalism, grounded in democratic practices and self-government and divorced from a reliance on a dogmatic free market, introduced the possibility of innovation and movement into social life:

> Socialism, grasped in its essential aspect, is the progressive actualization of the idea of liberty and justice among men.... Liberalism in its most straightforward sense can be defined as the political theory that takes the inner freedom of the human spirit as a given and adopts liberty as the ultimate goal, but also the ultimate means, the ultimate rule, of shared human life... in which each individual is certain of being able to develop his own personality fully.... Liberalism conceives of liberty not as a fact of nature, but as becoming, as development. One is not born free; one becomes free. And one stays free by retaining an active and vigilant sense of one's autonomy, by constantly exercising one's freedoms... in the name of liberty, [socialists] want social life to be guided not by the egoistic criterion of personal utility, but by the social criterion, the criterion of the collective good.

The accord with British liberals' ideas of individual development, the social moulding of personality, the quest for a common good, and the assertion that communal life is at the disposal of the individual—as well as a resonance with the deep spirituality of Croce—is striking.

John Dewey (1859–1952), the American philosopher and educationalist, was a liberal theorist reacting to a cultural environment quite dissimilar to those of his European counterparts. To begin with, 20th century American liberalism was an unusual combination of progressivism and nationalism, notably articulated in the writings of Herbert Croly. At the same time, the connotations of liberalism in the USA can be more negative than anything to be found in European democracies, signifying as they did—in the wake of the New Deal of the 1930s—big, interventionist government that in the worst case saps individual initiative and independence, or, alternatively, undermines the ability to take a strong position in political altercations. Dewey belonged to the school of philosophical thought known as Pragmatism and his approach, as expressed in particular in his *Liberalism and Social Action*, was strongly experimental and based on experience. Liberalism was in his view a practical set of ideas, historically conditioned and relative, rather than containing universal immutable truths that had to be uncovered.

Dewey resisted the distinction between the individual and political society. Although he hailed the significance of British philosophers such as Green and his successors in proclaiming the ideals of liberalism to be the common good, liberty, individuality, and the claim of each individual to the full development of his or her capacities, Dewey maintained that liberal values were the outcome of concrete collective activity. It was human intelligence, not an abstract spiritual essence, that propelled liberalism:

> A liberal program has to be developed, and in a good deal of particularity, outside of the immediate realm of governmental action and enforced upon public attention, before direct political action of a thorough-going liberal sort will follow... the majority who call themselves liberals today are committed to the principle that organized society must use its powers to establish the conditions under which the mass of individuals can possess actual as distinct from merely legal liberty.

In bringing liberalism down to earth, Dewey humanized it and freed it from the rigid, doctrinaire constraints that both natural rights theory and political economy had imposed on it in the past.

Liberalism required the inclusion of economic activities, but in his stringent critique of capitalism Dewey argued that they had to be subordinated to the higher capacities of individuals. Indeed, the initiative and vigour channelled through economic life was mistakenly assumed to apply to economics alone, to the exclusion of their presence in 'companionship, science and art'. Not least, Dewey's insistence on the inextricability of individual action from human association was reminiscent of Hobhouse's pairing of mutual aid and mutual forbearance, and the organic interdependence of society that demanded 'collective social planning'. Dewey's empiricism also identified another feature of liberalism—albeit shared with other ideologies—towards which Hobhouse had been working his way in less explicit form: the emotional intensity of liberal ideas was necessary to bring them to fruition. Reason alone was ineffective in a political ideology, even in liberalism, unless it was sustained by passion.

This chapter ends with an assessment of the ideas of Friedrich August von Hayek (1899–1992), an economist, philosopher, and political thinker who was awarded the Nobel Prize in economics in 1974. To be sure, Hayek is a controversial figure in the annals of liberalism. One thing he certainly illustrates is the continuing struggle over the intellectual heritage of liberals. Whether Hayek is considered a liberal (which he insisted he was), a conservative, a libertarian, or a hybrid among those, is itself a question of ideological as well as scholarly interpretation, and it is one to which Hayek contributed an active role. That role is expressed on two levels: in his own account of the history of liberalism, and in the substantive arguments he produced about liberalism and the place of liberty within it.

For Hayek, the heyday of liberalism was in the mid-19th century. In an instructive article he contributed to the Italian *Enciclopedia del Novecento* he rejected Croce's distinction between *liberalismo* and *liberismo*, claiming instead that freedom under the law simply implied economic freedom for individuals. Liberal freedom was—contra Green—a negative conception referring to the absence of an evil, the evil of government directing the individual towards particular ends and benefits. Hence, argued Hayek, liberalism began to decline from the 1870s, since which time—and particularly under the new liberalism at the beginning of the 20th century—'new experiments in social policy were undertaken which were only doubtfully compatible with the older liberal principles'. Those older principles were the ones towards which Hayek was deeply sympathetic. Welfare liberalism was interpreted as a departure from liberal principles, which for Hayek involved the cluster of liberty, law, and property, while he dismissed the belief in progress as 'the sign of a shallow mind.'

We encounter here the perennial problem of change over time. Is liberalism—or for that matter any ideology—a set of fundamental beliefs, a doctrine with an original exemplar from which there are deplorable deviations, or is it a continuously evolving and changing set of ideas around a loose core of values, as Dewey saw it? Hayek plumped firmly for the former. His resistance to the mutation of ideas was different, however, from that of those philosophers—recently, John Rawls and Ronald Dworkin come to mind—who identify a pure, abstract principle at the centre of liberalism. For Hayek, rather, it was a matter of tried and tested experience examining which claim to liberalism had worked best, but, once that question was settled, it was no longer open to alteration.

The centrality of liberty to Hayek's work followed from what he believed was the natural spontaneity of human beings and a socio-economic order that was self-generating: Hayek referred to that kind of order as a catallaxy. Human knowledge was dispersed and could not be possessed by any single directing authority, including the state. The central direction of all economic activity according to a single plan or blueprint would catastrophically eliminate the purposiveness and rationality of innovating individuals, and impoverish the exchange of ideas—indeed, the market of ideas—that could be put to the service of a society. That was the energizing and optimistic component of layer two liberalism that Hayek embraced. Individual freedom was thus essential for economic and social flourishing, as progress could not be centrally engineered, and social justice was a contradiction in terms. Hayek borrowed the phrase 'open society' to describe his position. In terms of a broader approach to liberalism, he expanded the spatial presence of the concept of liberty within the liberal core—spelt out in Chapter 4—at the expense of most liberal core concepts. The only other core segments Hayek retained were limited, constitutional power and a specific notion of individuality as experimental innovation.

> Liberalism ... merely demands that the procedure, or the rules of the game, by which the relative positions of the different individuals are determined, be just (or at least not unjust), but not that the particular results of this process for the different individuals be just...
>
> The central belief from which all liberal postulates may be said to spring is that the more successful solutions of the problems of society are to be expected if we do not rely on the application of anyone's given knowledge, but encourage the interpersonal process of the exchange of opinion from which better knowledge can be expected to emerge.

Chapter 6
Philosophical liberalism: idealizing justice

Basic postulates

There is another, parallel and partially separate, world of liberal thinking and theorizing, one that takes place almost wholly within the walls of academe. Liberal political philosophy is a particular sub-set of liberal language. Though with strong roots in English philosophical traditions, its more recent manifestations have, broadly speaking, been American. They resonate with the constitutional arrangements peculiar to the USA and, assisted by the worldwide power of American publishing and the opulence of its leading universities, have often, and mistakenly, been thought to represent liberalism as a whole. More to the point, liberal political philosophy now constitutes the major creative and probing instance of current liberal theorizing even as, ironically, the vernacular connotations of liberalism are under frequent attack in broader American political discourse. The previous period of liberal flourishing took place a century ago among the new and left liberals in the UK, but it was far more immersed in actual political life and reform and served as an apposite example of what action-oriented and group-supported political ideologies are like. If Chapter 3 engaged with liberalism as a set of discontinuous, overlapping, and reinforcing concrete and politically engaged histories, the political impact of philosophical liberalism is partly disabled by its fundamental premises. It is largely an abstract and ideal-type normative approach invoking an ostensibly supra-political, universal, and decontextualized social ethics towards which all right-minded individuals should aim. Admittedly, there has also been another 20th century flourishing of ideas claiming to be liberal, neoliberalism, but those claims are questionable, as we will see in Chapter 7.

Philosophical liberalism presents arguments for the construction of legitimate and ethically attractive social arrangements, focusing on a number of central areas. It is, first, predominantly preoccupied with the shaping of a just society. Second, it assumes individuals to be rational, autonomous, and purposive agents and it is designed to promote those attributes. Third, it seeks out justifications for a decent society that all its members can endorse. It does so by emphasizing large-scale involvement in decision-making, and it holds out the prospect of outline consensus on communal policy based on an appeal to human rationality and fairness. Fourth, many of its articulations have a specific take on the state, to which it entrusts the securing of the political end of neutrality among the different conceptions of the good held by its citizens.

All this means that people must be offered the opportunity to express their preferences through a threefold process. First, individuals should be given not only the vote but a voice. They should be encouraged to articulate their views clearly, without hindrance. Second, they should be persuaded to play a role in public life so that they can control their own fates. Hence active political participation has to be promoted. Third, they should respect others in the same manner in which they wish to be respected—that is called recognition. Recognition has symbolic value in accepting the uniqueness, dignity, and worth of individuals, but it also has material consequences for the allocation of possessions and benefits. All those liberal principles are there to be discovered through the exercise of reason and ethical intuitions.

Philosophic liberalism is strongly universalistic and unafraid to postulate moral truths. It does not see itself as one amongst many ideological creeds competing for primacy but as a prescription for the good life of individuals and a civilized life for a society, in essence above the contingencies of the political fray. It is in effect a system of high-minded morality—indeed, on that view liberalism is simply identical to a social ethics that is insulated from politics. It has, however, impressively developed a persuasive force of its own that has often overtaken more vernacular expressions of liberalism and—at least among the more cerebral liberal aficionados—put those expressions in the shade.

Not all of this is new. For centuries such analytical-philosophical models have anchored liberalism in a frame of desirable human conduct with instant, universal rational appeal that ostensibly decontextualizes it and detaches it from the vagaries of life. Social contract theory established grounds for founding a political society anchored in certain ideas about human nature as reasonable and conflict-averse. Psychological approaches to human flourishing stipulated that the maximizing urge to self-benefit could be harnessed to a society useful to all. But liberal political philosophy has undergone an extraordinary flowering in recent decades as a minor intellectual industry. It is particularly adept at generating thought experiments to initiate schemes for the fair distribution of crucial goods. Those experiments hypothesize what risk-averse individuals would want for themselves and others if they were originally ignorant about their social circumstances, and about most of their capacities.

Rawls's philosophical laboratory

The leading and most influential theorist of philosophical liberalism in the 20th century was John Rawls (1921–2002). Rawls's famous phrase, 'justice is the first virtue of social institutions' has had significant resonance in recalibrating liberal values. In other liberal variants that first virtue might be liberty, or privacy, or well-being, or progress, or individuality. For Rawls the essence of liberalism lies in two components, the one libertarian and the other egalitarian. The libertarian component aspires to make individuals more capable of making choices about their lives that are not only free, but reflective and sensible. That component is the autonomy conception of liberty mentioned in Chapter 4. The egalitarian component is Rawls's most creative contribution to liberal theory. It insists on satisfying basic conditions for social justice; that is to say, endowing individuals with the requisite resources without which they will not have the effective possibility of pursuing autonomous ends and living a good life of their choosing. That entails not only ensuring the equal liberty of all members of a society, but a redistribution of goods designed to benefit the least advantaged, who have prior claim on wealth and services before others can benefit from them. To the extent that individual circumstances are the consequence of brute luck, the argument goes, the less fortunate should be compensated in a just society. That luck might be genetic, or reflect the fertility of a geographical region, or relate to the means possessed by the family into which one is born. However, the 'least advantaged' remains an elusive category as a policy guide as it is consummately difficult to identify an individual who would occupy that hapless position simultaneously on the different scales of wealth, health, intelligence, and good looks, to mention some of the more prominent criteria that determine human life-chances. Because we may be advantaged on one scale and deprived on another, this requires a comparison that can never be conclusive.

It is no accident that in his version of liberalism Rawls makes a move from justice to fairness. Replacing the grandiloquent connotations of justice for a society as a whole, Rawls approaches justice more modestly as building up from a personal, small-scale reflection on how any individual would want to be treated fairly and applying that reflection to all. He employs a thought-experiment that relies on methodological individualism, that is to say, on positing the individual alone as the unit of analysis, abstracted from his or her social environment. In what Rawls terms the 'original position', each individual is placed under a veil of ignorance about most of their characteristics, about their position in society, about the groups to which they belong, and about their life-chances. However, even under that veil individuals are still endowed with two features: they are rational and they are risk-averse. In addition, individuals possess two pre-social moral powers: a sense of justice and a conception of the good. Equipped with those attributes they are expected to determine what each of them would want both for themselves and for others. For Rawls, that is the optimal approach to exploring what a fair political system should look like.

The second moral power involves the capacity of individuals to form, revise, and pursue a conception of one's rational advantage or good, though it bypasses the fact that alternative liberal viewpoints increasingly accept that people are also motivated by emotional and irrational factors. As will be illustrated in Chapter 7, emotion is part and parcel of thought and conduct, even within the liberal family. Philosophical liberals are keen to see individuals working intellectually, and especially morally, at full strength. They pay little heed to the human frailty that welfare state liberals incorporated into their thinking or to the passions that motivate people, passions that sometimes reinforce but at other times undercut their moral sensibilities. Arguably, few individuals are inclined to shoulder the burden of repeatedly re-assessing their life plans, a point brilliantly made in 1907 by Herbert Asquith, about to become the British Liberal prime minister, who had attended T.H. Green's lectures but reacted sceptically to that philosopher's message by commenting: 'I believe in the right of every man face to face with the State to make the best of himself and subject to the limitation that he does not become a nuisance or a danger to the community to make less than the best of himself.' For Rawls, nonetheless, the impact of the two moral powers under the veil of ignorance is to create a fair order of free and equal persons acting as fully cooperating members of a society. The endemic presence of conflict and dissent is minimized because rational collaboration is elevated to the default position of social life—it is the norm of human conduct.

The egalitarian component of liberalism—rarely, and if so implicitly, at the core of the older liberal layers—has been moved to centre-stage in many recent philosophical arguments because a liberal society is now held to be one that guarantees each and every member generous access to important social goods. That liberal egalitarianism usually falls short of the radical equalization of socialist schemes. It rests content with ensuring minima for a humane life, and with reducing the gap between the fortunate and the disadvantaged through a mix of public and private redistributive measures—the state, employers' codes of conduct, and voluntary associations such as charities. But it is prepared to permit discrepancies in wealth that will nonetheless influence life-chances. Undoubtedly, there is plausibility in the Rawlsian precepts as a characterization of liberalism's actual and historical preconditions and ends, given the many possible meanings of liberty, equality, and justice in the liberal family. But this, more than most other liberal schemes, is primarily a stipulative vision (or what Rawls occasionally termed a 'realistic utopia') of the arrangements that any fair and decent society should seek to implement. Notably current philosophers, unlike many of their political theory counterparts, are prone to referring to liberalism in the singular, not the plural. They see no need for argument about its interpretation and priorities. It is conceived of as the distillation of the agreed normative requirements of a free and well-ordered community, and one that will ensure its long-term stability.

Left-liberalism and ideal-type liberalism

Rawlsian philosophical liberalism shares certain similarities with fourth layer liberalism. Both subscribe to a strong idea of internal harmony and consensus on which all right-thinking people will converge. And both place considerable emphasis on social policies that will work in favour of the marginalized and underprivileged members of a society. But there the similarities end. Philosophical liberalism in its Rawlsian version is based on hypothetical assumptions that model human thought and conduct, and are therefore immediately attainable in a specific, imagined, and context-free thought exercise. Fourth layer liberalism was the outcome of actual and hard-won radical policies, however imperfect, that saw the slow rise of a welfare society in a piecemeal and gradual process. Notably, Rawls's analysis is based on an individual artificially insulated from the social groups that fourth layer liberals regarded as contributing significantly to individual ability and character, due to his belief that the veil of ignorance can usefully model human conduct and form the basis for social arrangements.

The strong individualism of much contemporary philosophical liberalism has also been put at the service of dichotomizing liberalism and communitarianism. It involves a sharp distinction between the emphasis on rational individuals capable of realizing themselves independently and a focus on the social anchoring of individuals—be that in a small group, a neighbourhood, or society as a whole. That dichotomy ignores the extent to which the liberal tradition, particularly in its social liberal mode—a mode of which many philosophical liberals seem to be unaware—reconciled the two tendencies. The decontextualized timelessness of philosophical liberalism, and its indifference to history, play down the importance of mutating social relationships in constituting the individual. Philosophical liberalism also treats as largely irrelevant the evidence that liberalism is an ideology that has had to struggle with other ideologies for supremacy and impact, and that liberalism undergoes continuous modifications when it emerges in different cultures. Seen historically and politically, liberalism has pursued an elusive universalism (or in more recent language, a globalism) intended to spread gradually—but far from completely—through example and expansion. On the contrary, the neatness of philosophical liberalism lies in its logical immediacy and robust persuasiveness for those who subscribe to its ethical vision. Once you accept its impeccable moral reasoning it simply becomes the correct viewpoint. Space and time offer no boundaries for ideal-type thinking. That is not offered as a critique of the enterprise of philosophical liberalism but as a comment on its different disciplinary allegiances.

What has to obtain for such a conception of liberalism to be workable? First, justice must be a universalizable idea that can be shared by all—there can be no multiple, ideologically competing, theories of justice possessing moral respectability. Second, human beings are unquestionably both moral and rational entities. For a Rawlsian philosophical liberal, there is an inevitability about human rationality that is morally compelling: being irrational is not an ethical option. Third, the sense of justice is based on an assumed overlapping consensus on universal ground rules, otherwise described as a theory of the right rather than of the good, because it over-rides procedurally the substantive religious, philosophical, and moral differences that invariably exist among people. That overlapping consensus is also 'free-standing'; in other words, it is not dependent on a more comprehensive liberal ideology of the kind this book has investigated—or any other ideology for that matter. However, Rawls does concede that it has an affinity with particular practices that are embedded in current democracies. Put differently, it just happens to be the case that each rational individual on his or her own will arrive at the same justifiable ethical ground rules. And it just happens to be the case that the resulting overlapping consensus is remarkably similar to some Western democratic assumptions. That consensus becomes the vital sustainer of social and constitutional stability, which, for Rawlsians, are also central political ends of liberalism.

The kind of pared-down 'political liberalism' advanced by Rawls has been criticized as far too minimal and out of step with other liberalisms purporting to contain radical messages. Two of its features have been singled out as inadequate. First, it does not include individuality, and possibly not even progress, at the centre of its vision. Second, its emphasis on what is uniquely human—a range of mental and moral capabilities—seriously understates the emotional and physical attributes of human beings, which are not necessarily captured on an ethically normative register. It is only when we take all four of those capabilities together as having robust claims on social policy that we can realize the welfare state liberalism that marked the policies of many 20th century European societies. Conversely, it is doubtful whether Rawls's 'thin' political liberalism can be universalized and made compatible with other ideologies or with all major religious belief systems.

Liberal neutrality

Other philosophical liberals have brought their own brands of liberal argumentation to the table. Their insistence on liberal neutrality is incompatible with a view of ideologies as a particular assemblage of decontested concepts, values, and preferences. It perpetuates the possibility of a clear divide between the private and the public, with the state abstaining from declaring a position on private matters. Liberal critics have found that divide increasingly controversial, not least because what one perspective finds private—hate speech or family relationships—another may find of public concern. Moreover, state silence effectively condones whatever the prevailing practice is, whether desirable or not. Unquestionably, liberals believe that many areas of human activity should be exempt from state control or regulation, but to make that a rigid rule would permit serious abuses to be disregarded.

For a while in the late 20th century a doctrine of liberal neutrality was a firm favourite among liberal philosophers, exemplified by Ronald Dworkin (1931–2013) with the American constitutional model in mind. The argument for state neutrality could only hold if certain choices, rules, and rights were regarded as supra-political, beyond human contention. That would seemingly limit liberalism's role not only to protecting all privately held values, however distasteful, but to the active facilitation of their expression, reminiscent of the old adage 'sticks and stones may break my bones, but words will never hurt me'. That approach is redolent of an older liberal view of harm as physical and legal rather than psychological and emotional.

Characteristically, Dworkin maintained that the great merit of the American Bill of Rights—the first ten amendments addition to the original American Constitution—was its decisive removal of certain fundamental principles from the control of democratic majorities. That was elaborated in Rawls's insistence on the urgent political requirement 'to fix, once and for all, the content of certain basic political rights and liberties', thus taking them off the political agenda. While understandable as an attempt to safeguard some liberal principles, that insistence is as elitist and political as many other expressions of liberal ideology. On that view, majorities tend to impose preferences on others and potentially violate individual rights, and those crucial rights need to be isolated from the vicissitudes that rule the political sphere by enshrining them in a constitution that is very hard to modify. The American Constitution and its Bill of Rights unquestionably include important liberal political practices, in particular establishing the principles of representation and the equal treatment of all citizens. But the immunity bestowed on the Bill of Rights has fostered the illusion that the Supreme Court possesses a neutral perspective impervious to political vicissitudes.

There are two reasons why that supra-political and non-partisan interpretation cannot hold. First, when viewed through the lens of ideological analysis, there is no view from nowhere. Every view embodies cultural, social, and personal predilections. Second, the Supreme Court itself does not assign equal value to all views—it harbours pretty clear ideas for what count as just practices.

Ideologies are always expressions of specific preferences for the good life, and consequently they rank what they believe is valuable in social practices and what isn't. That ranking is always a political act. The argument against neutrality asserts that the Bill of Rights was itself the outcome of a particular constellation of ideas, ideologies, and cultural inclinations, and hence far from being a neutral guarantor of socially valuable goods. On that view, liberalism is a culturally parochial ideology—however attractive—masquerading as a universal one. As a predominantly European and North American cluster of ideas, liberalism has been exported to Latin America and to other countries, but always through local cultural filters. However, that view of liberalism was dismissed by Dworkin and his supporters as a sociological argument, not a philosophical one. In fact, it is neither, but an insight emanating from the comparative analysis of liberal ideologies, a project whose methodological openness is itself liberal.

Philosophical liberals find it hard to conceive of rights to liberty, to equality of respect, or to due process as themselves impositions on the conduct of others, or as a choice of specific values out of a larger pool, because they hold such rights to be the universal, logical, and ethical outcome of social life. That said, neutrality is itself a positive concept that has been promoted in some liberal quarters. Liberals who profess neutrality are far from neutral in recommending it—indeed they can be passionate about neutrality—and in that context advocating neutrality is a contradiction in terms. Better to hope for Supreme Court impartiality—addressing questions of justice and rights without favour or bias. Impartiality may be distinguished from neutrality, as it may be pursued within a framework that is itself non-neutral about the virtue of law and the wickedness of crime. That possibility is nevertheless difficult to sustain when one considers the frequently blatant partisan nature of Supreme Court nominations, even taking into account that the Justices are constrained by the rules and ethos of legal procedure. More broadly, as Herbert Croly noted in the evolutionary language prevalent a century ago, 'whether in any particular case the state takes sides or remains impartial, it most assuredly has a positive function to perform on the premises. If it remains impartial, it simply agrees to abide by the results of natural selection.' These problems once again illustrate the considerable tensions between purist, ideal-type, and abstract liberal philosophizing on the one hand and contextual views of liberalism that locate it in a spatial and temporal domain on the other. That domain reflects human design with all its strengths and fallibilities through the mirrors of disparate cultures and varying historical eras. That counter-approach is a rival approach to the philosophical study of political ideas. There is no need to rule on which approach is the more valid or persuasive, merely to recognize the diverse premises that vindicate the one or the other.

The standards of public life

Another theme in contemporary philosophical liberalism diverts it from realizing the long-standing ideological core of liberalism in its various guises. The emphasis switches to developing practices that give politics a good name and that reverse the often dubious reputation with which politics as a whole has been saddled. Liberalism is consequently repackaged as providing strong and specific standards that guide the proper ways those active in the public domain should conduct themselves. Foremost among those public guidelines are the need to display transparency and accountability, to counter corruption and complacency, and to justify public policy in a manner that can reach out to all members of society. All those address liberal core ideas in an oblique manner. The American political theorist Gerald Gaus has identified this as the requirement for public reason that ensures a 'genuinely liberal political life', and the British philosopher Bernard Williams as a 'basic legitimacy demand'—one that insists that the state offer a justification of its power to each subject, although that itself is an impossibly idealist prerequisite. The high premium apportioned by many political theorists to fostering articulate deliberation as the bedrock of democratic practice, and to encouraging public accessibility to conversations among political elites, upholds those approaches. They exhibit a palpable shift from a liberalism whose aim it is to protect the virtues of the private sphere to one whose aim it is to vitalize the public sphere, continuing a process that began well over a century ago but playing down other established liberal ends.

The liberal core concepts of the general interest, of rationality and of limited power still underpin this philosophical dialogue, but more as indicators of decent and civilized conduct than as the distillation of substantive values that direct liberal policy. Notably, as Gaus puts it, the view he represents regards politics as the 'continuation of ethics by other means'. The problem with this view is that it undermines politics as an autonomous area of human thought and action, and raises expectations of the political sphere as an impartial adjudicating arena of morality and virtue, one that liberalism simply cannot deliver. A more realistically grounded and flexible liberalism, a liberalism both principled and sceptical, might question that. Liberalism, to repeat, has throughout its history actively promoted certain choices and has regarded some features of public life as non-negotiable, dependent neither on consensus nor on adjudication. The bottom line is that no ideology, liberalism included, can forego the self-assumed responsibility of introducing its certainties into political life. Politics always includes that drive to finality on an ideology's own terms, even when it is doomed to failure or to partial realization.

Liberal philosophical pluralism

There is another form of liberal philosophizing, one of whose leading exponents was the British philosopher Isaiah Berlin (1909–97). Berlin held that values were plural and diverse, and therefore could not be ranked in relation to each other. On the surface this bears some resemblance to the fifth layer of liberal pluralism, but it is in fact an older kind of pluralism. Rather than being based on notions of group identity held by groups themselves, it relates to the moral diversity of human values and of the choices people are entitled to make. The problem with according equal respect to the values held by individuals is that it bypasses the empirical fact that ranking goods is an inevitable feature of political life. Without a means of distributing the significance of values and asserting that 'this is more important, or worthy, than that' no political decisions can be taken. As a philosophical observation Berlin's insistence on the incommensurability of values has some appeal to liberals (though even then most of them safeguard specific values through bestowing on them the finality of rights). As a political characterization, however, it does not represent actual liberalisms, which have to compete for their fortunes in the public arena in their quest to control political language.

Berlin, however, appreciated that conflict was inescapable, and his disdain for totalitarianism and the monism it entailed justified in his view a strong preference for the liberty of each individual to be different, rather than the alternative liberty of converging on universal rational truths and on ethical harmony. Here again a tension is evident: that between the decontested values and preferences that all ideologies exhibit and the desire to open up the range of human expression without hindrance. When liberals express support for the core concepts identified in Chapter 4, they try to choose certain conceptions of each concept in a manner that will permit a high degree of compatibility among them. At the same time, their preferences for those particular decontestations, and their dislike of others, shape their views of the political and moral worlds they inhabit. Liberals may be more amenable to the flexibility and adjustability of those conceptual clusters, but not infinitely so. Berlin preached toleration, but even liberal toleration has its no-go areas. Berlin himself, of course, subscribed to his own ranking of values, one in which (negative) liberty was a master concept. He was therefore intolerant of attempts to undermine it. When push comes to shove, a ranking of preferences must be arrived at in each concrete instance of governing and communal living. That is the flipside of liberal philosophers' espousal of neutrality. Rather, as Berlin insisted, the one-size-fits-all of universal solutions disregards the 'crooked timber of humanity'. That is why the right to, and capacity for, moral as well as political choice occupied pride of place in his kind of liberalism, even when the actual choices could be misguided.

Philosophical liberalism is a complex field of argument, assessment, and ideational experimentation. No creed can survive and remain healthy without the constant infusion of critical thinking from within. Political philosophers have pushed forward the boundaries of liberalism by subjecting it to intense scrutiny and they have also repeatedly attempted to tackle pressing issues of immense social significance—What has to happen for a political system to be legitimate? When is civil disobedience justified? What makes an individual deserving of rewards in the form of social goods? Should we compensate individuals for misfortune? Which democratic practices are most conducive to sustaining democracy? How do we reconcile cultural and ethnic loyalties with free choice and individuality? Philosophical liberalism has frequently narrowed and defined the area in which answers to questions such as these can—and should—be found. But to the extent that some of its practitioners believe in clear solutions to those issues, they may find themselves crossing the admittedly porous line between liberalism and its challengers—particularly that between the utopias of human perfection and the liberal acknowledgement of imperfection.

Chapter 7
Misappropriations, disparagements, and lapses

Ideologies are precarious and volatile things. They may burst out of their reasonable confines. They may fall into the wrong political hands and be abused. They may suffer from hubris and become an embarrassment to many of their adherents. They may lose touch with political reality. Or they may pull a metaphorical rabbit out of a hat and deliver far more than was expected of them. Liberalism ticks every one of those boxes.

In the debate over the question 'is liberalism the winning ideology?' one major issue is obscured. The rhetorical use of the word 'liberalism' is common in some circles that are not obviously liberal; all too often, they employ liberalism in a lax, restricted, and particularly tendentious fashion that serves their own ideological purposes. One intention may be to take cover under the umbrella of liberalism in order to sweeten some unpleasant pills those non-liberals are keen for people to swallow. Many right-wing and populist parties have gone down that route in recent years. Another intention may be to create a hostile caricature of liberalism—a foil against which it is easier to argue contrary positions. That route is often taken by Marxists or by postmodern thinkers.

The neoliberal offensive

As alluded to in earlier chapters, one of the most prominent misrepresentations of liberalism has been the introduction of the term 'neoliberalism'. In this case an ideological variant dons the mantle of a rival in order to clothe itself in rhetorical respectability and even to wrest ground, deliberately or unwittingly, away from established liberal versions. Neoliberals tend to see the world as an immense and potentially unencumbered global market, in which the exchange of goods for profit overrides other aspects of cross-national relations. Individual understandings of neoliberalism will of course differ. But in general terms, being a liberal is understood by neoliberals to characterize the free individual agent, alone or in conjunction with others, as being above all economically assertive. The defining features of that assertiveness are to maintain and develop the economic power inherent in capitalist production and transactions, to open up new areas for investment, and to benefit from the plethora of goods available for consumption. Neoliberals subordinate social, political, and cultural spheres to a professed self-regulating economic market and their principles are supposed to inspire the ways all social activities are run.

In terms of liberal morphology, neoliberals confine the core liberal concept of rationality to maximizing economic advantage. They do away with any idea of natural sociability and minimize mention of human individuality as the end of social progress. State power is mainly marshalled to guaranteeing trade and commerce, not to creating the conditions for human flourishing and well-being. Instead the unfettered power of the market is unleashed, so that the liberal concept of constrained and accountable power is circumvented. It is retained mainly to protect entrepreneurs in going about their business, while sidestepping the aim of a genuinely free market that could unlock the economic energy and inventiveness held to be intrinsic to all individuals. In its most recent forms, neoliberalism champions a world in which huge multinational corporations and mega-banks increasingly control and dictate the way we live, fostering an imposed and conformist managerialism. Instead of regarding economic intercourse as a means to the furthering of political ends such as peace and international solidarity, it sees political institutions as a framework arrangement for securing the efficiency and financial prosperity of the private sector. Liberal universalism has been replaced with neoliberal globalism; the ethical permeation of individuals has been supplanted by the economic ingestion of territory. Even governments themselves are predominantly recast as investors and facilitators of trade, rather than deliverers of welfare or social justice. Only when financial crises erupt do governments make efforts to regulate the world of banking, but that is done with a relatively light touch.

In promoting the notion of a self-regulating market, neoliberals approach conservative terrain. One of conservatism's key features is a belief in the extra-human origins of the social order, reflecting sets of rules that derive from the divine, the historical, the economic, or the 'natural'. Neoliberals provide a self-assured economic version of the naturally balanced system. In that version, attempts to direct and coordinate human effort can trigger catastrophic intervention when 'natural' economic rules are flouted. Hayek's inspiration is evident on this point. In terms of liberalism's layers, neoliberalism has been decoupled from its closest antecedent, layer two market liberalism, which nourished a moral vision of markets as a part of a civilizing endeavour, emphasizing individual talent not corporate power. There are few vestiges of an ethical mission towards a fair society among neoliberals—instead, levels of social inequality have been rising under neoliberal policies. And there is little commitment to engaging the engines of progress in the quest for human self-improvement. The welfare-state role of layer four is whittled away or handed over to private organizations. The constitutional arrangements of layer one, with their safeguarding of individual space and liberation from tyranny, are retained but effectively redirected towards free competition among powerful and vastly unequal economic players. In sum, neoliberals do not possess the minimum kit to be located squarely at the heart of 21st century liberalism. Put more forcefully, the complex morphology of liberalism is shattered and becomes barely recognizable.

East European liberalism after 1989

One intriguing aspect of neoliberalism has been its attractiveness to a number of former communist countries following the collapse of the Soviet Union in the early 1990s. In the absence of a strong liberal tradition in those countries it was hardly surprising that garbled versions of liberalism took hold in Poland, Hungary, and the Czech Republic. What in fact went under the name of liberalism pulled in two very different directions. The already weak manifestations of liberalism in Eastern Europe suffered an identity crisis in the post-communist search for new identities: its emblematic defence of individual liberty and social solidarity were consigned to civil society, while its equally characteristic championing of competition and private property were the province of a market society. The two parts shared little and were made to lead separate institutional and ideological lives.

The appeal of neoliberalism was understandable in countries whose economies had suffered under communism. The personal circumstances of most citizens made a consumer society on imagined 'Western' models of opulence particularly alluring. Citizens were prompted to search for a more efficient economic system whose fruits were tangible and immediate, and neoliberalism seemed to hold out the prospect of a fast fix. But the other direction some East European countries took was a flight from the oppressive and dictatorial states under which people had lived. Here liberals genuinely had to make up lost ground for the many decades endured under totalitarian systems, in particular the absence of robust, basic first layer constraints and procedures. The liberal language of human rights and of bringing back the

5. Shortly before becoming Czech president in December 1989, Václav Havel waves to crowds in Prague celebrating freedom after the collapse of communism.

rule of law and democratic constitutional arrangements was in the mouths of many (Figure 5). As against the powerful state under communism, many liberals pinned their hopes on the strengthening of civil society as a refuge from the state. 'Civil society' was the prevalent term for the network of voluntary and private associations that made up society, in the civic and cultural as well as the economic spheres.

In that soil, fourth layer welfare liberalism, relying as it did on the benevolence of an active and democratic state, but a state nonetheless, could hardly flourish. Both civil society and market society tendencies shared the quest to diminish the centrality of the state as far as possible, whether it acted for good or for evil. The state, in the words of the Polish academic Jerzy Szacki, was seen 'as the agent of all social injustice', a position quite out of step with left-liberal ideological and philosophical theories. Collective action was mistakenly identified with the socialist collectivism of the old regimes. Anything even remotely associated with collectivism was thus to be avoided.

The belief in the harmonious functioning of civil society without some state regulation amidst the complexities of the modern world was naive and illusory, as it previously had been in liberalism's past history, when private and charitable institutions proved unable to provide solutions to the social problems of the 19th century. Indeed, neoliberalism now illustrated once again how dominant private interests merely moved in to fill the power vacuum caused by bypassing the state. At the same time, visions of civil society in Eastern Europe demanded levels of social homogeneity that fifth layer multicultural liberals would consider utopian and regard with suspicion. And the misleading idea that civil society was a parallel society, happily separate from the distasteful world of politics, implied that political issues did not permeate the whole of society. The discrete notions of the state, the government, and politics were frequently and carelessly equated. Liberalism failed to take deeper roots in Eastern Europe, while its ideas of liberty were pressed into personalized and idealized intellectual and artistic spheres.

The pseudo-liberals

Although neoliberals may genuinely, if misguidedly, believe that they are the most important heirs to the liberal tradition, other societies—especially in Europe—have produced ideologies that knowingly obscure their credentials. They dress themselves up in a pseudo-liberal discourse that is laid bare, like the emperor's new clothes, the moment we apply the morphological approach to ideologies.

The deliberate misappropriation of liberalism can become a political weapon designed to mask the true intentions of an ideology or to render its rhetoric more palatable. The right-wing

Austrian Freedom Party, for example, has exploited the liberal language of economic freedoms to disguise another kind of 'freedom' it is pushing: that of the nation's emancipation from foreigners and large-scale immigration. In the Netherlands, the List Pim Fortuyn combined a tolerant attitude to homosexuality with strong anti-Islamic and xenophobic policies. Its successor—named 'The Freedom Party' in the same populist tradition of obfuscation—continues with resistance to the integration of immigrants alongside a condemnation of layer five social pluralism. In all those cases the most valued liberty is that of promoting what is claimed to be a dominant national culture, while demonizing people from different ethnic groups. As the well-known adage has it, just as one swallow does not make a summer, so one or two liberal-sounding ideas do not constitute liberalism—especially when blatantly illiberal ideas are deliberately stacked behind them.

The relative success of liberalism, and the tolerance and openness of its most humanistic versions, makes it an easy target for ideological scavengers and the object of permanent attack from crusading or populist movements. Liberalism's own integrity is not helped by the different faces it presents to the world or, indeed, by the complexity of arguments it marshals when, to the contrary, political action demands simplification. But that is the common fate of any ideology that seeks to compete over the control of political language.

Liberal internationalism

Whereas neoliberalism is rarely seen by its critics as part of the liberal family, there is another area that has fashioned its own take on liberalism. This is not a case of misappropriation but of trimming and recasting. Over the past half-century or so, the language of international relations has repeatedly referred to a 'liberal world order'. The proponents of that view are prone to a macro view of liberalism in which broad contours are adumbrated but the fine distinguishing details that identify an ideology as liberal are elided. As Georg Sørensen has observed, 'Liberal ideas about the international sphere are less developed than liberal ideas about domestic politics'. Whereas liberal ideas and ideologies in domestic settings are both complex and frequently challenged and criticized by other ideologies, competing as they do against conservative, nationalist, socialist, green, fundamentalist, or populist tendencies, there is paradoxically a large degree of consensus among international relations analysts that the world order is a liberal one. Yet it is difficult to talk of a recognizably liberal world order emanating from the so-called 'West' and underpinned in particular by the nigh-hegemonic status of the USA. For that international order is supported and often aggressively promoted on a micro level by conservative, nationalist, and quasi-populist governments as well as by social-democratic welfare states, none of which falls happily into the liberal camp as seen by the discerning analyst of ideologies.

What, then, is a 'liberal world order' and why is the term so popular both among many players in the international arena and among international relations experts? At its heart are three assumptions, explicit or implicit. First, that 'liberal-democracy' refers not to an ideology but to a type of regime, to a set of institutional political arrangements and a rule-based system for which the phrase 'liberal-democracy' is a useful abbreviation. Those arrangements are mainly in line with the minimalist base that first layer liberalism advocates, but they lag far behind liberal transformations since the mid-19th century. It is now a commonplace for many conservative, social-democratic, nationalist, or populist systems—particularly in Europe and in the American continent, but also in Australia, New Zealand, India, and Japan—to accept constitutionalism and the rule of law without adopting ideologies that are notably or unambiguously liberal. The over-generalizing postulation that all those polities are liberal in their interactions leads theorists of international relations to contend that liberal principles are frequently violated in practice by liberal states.

It would be more plausible to maintain that so-called 'liberal states' do not necessarily possess either liberal governments or comprehensive liberal ideologies. Their practices may not be liberal to begin with because their liberalism is either nominal and thin or profoundly outbalanced by non-liberal ideas. To describe George W. Bush's foreign policy with regard to Iraq as promoting liberty and democracy in seeking forcibly to impose regime change does not imply that American policy was liberal under the highly conservative Republicans in any of the senses suggested by the third or fourth layers of liberalism. To the contrary, it risks disparaging liberalism as a whole. Even the promotion of liberty itself, described as a 'liberal impulse' in the international order, is no guarantee of membership of the liberal family if it entails, in R.H. Tawney's famous phrase, that 'freedom for the pike is death for the minnows'.

The second assumption is that liberalism always involves an economy based on capitalism and markets (an assumption to be distinguished from the exaggerated neoliberal inflating of free markets at the expense of most other liberal values). That is insufficiently nuanced, for neither capitalism nor markets are fixed quantities. They display degrees of control and regulation that vary vastly within different ideological frameworks. Some libertarians will be far more accommodating to free markets than welfare liberals. And some business entrepreneurs will be far more attuned to the profit motive than those liberals who wish to divert some of those profits—through taxation and other means—towards public and socially beneficial goods and services. As was seen in Chapter 4, incompatibility among liberal core concepts results in very different decontestations and orderings, often in direct competition with each other. If in the past private property was part of the ethos inherited from Locke and others, neither it nor capitalism itself—as a system of investment and expansion of financial and commercial power—have been specifically or uniquely liberal over the past century, contrary to the prevailing views of the liberal international order. Capitalism has been endorsed and pursued by non-liberal states such as China, as well as within European and American countries whose ideologies and regimes are, or were, patently not just conservative or socialist but nationalist or fascist.

The third assumption holds that to be liberal on the international scene is usually associated with the promotion of universal human rights and with peaceful conflict resolution. But there is divergence over which human rights should be protected and advanced, a divergence that parallels the difference between the first liberal layer on the one hand and the third and fourth on the other. The established list of human rights principally contains the rights of respect for individual freedom; protection from tyranny and torture; security; property ownership; and gender, race, and religious equality—and, collectively, of national self-determination. It was only subsequently that the United Nations and other international agencies attempted to shift the emphasis to the right to human development that is central to layer three, and to the relatively generous range of social and economic rights that is central to layer four.

Consequently, new notions of interventionism have now entered internationalist liberal discourse. Universal welfare considerations that were well-known to layer four liberals (the securing of conditions that prevent domestic humanitarian crises), have changed the rationale for intervention and enforcement, as for example in Kosovo, in Africa, and in the Middle East—albeit in selective and haphazard manner. However, there is no consensus among states or among students of international studies on prioritizing those additional rights or even on classifying them as liberal. The problem with accounts of liberal internationalism and with ascribing the adjective 'liberal' to the main agents committed to constructing a world order is not that they conceal the full view of liberalism, but that they do not seem to benefit from knowledge of the richness of liberal argument that has accrued over time and across space. Although that problem exists in some circles with respect to domestic liberalisms as well, it is much more prevalent in international politics.

Liberalism as culprit

One consistent stream of criticism of liberal premises, with the characteristic one-sidedness of ideological disputes, has originated in the Marxist camp. Marxists have regarded liberalism as a typical bourgeois ideology, furthering capitalist interests at the expense of the working class, or engaged in the abstract utopian promotion of human rights rather than the concrete advance of material conditions. H.J. Laski (1893–1950), the British writer and socialist who went through a Marxist phase, offers a good illustration. Laski acknowledged in passing the existence of left-liberal thinkers, such as T.H. Green or Hobhouse, and even praised the early liberal breakthroughs such as advancing freedom of contract. But liberalism 'forgot not less completely than its predecessors that the claims of social justice were not exhausted by its victory.' The historical institutions created by freedom 'veiled an internal decay':

> Liberalism has always been affected by its tendency to regard the poor as men who have failed through their own fault. It has always suffered from its inability to realize that great possessions mean power over men and women as well as over things.... Its purposes, no doubt, were always expressed in universal terms; but they were, in practical operation... the servant of a single class in the community.

In public political discourse in the United States liberalism is, from a very different stance, frequently—and dichotomously—paired with conservatism. Even professional analysts tend to work within the confines of that pairing. To suggest that Americans can simply be parcelled out between the two headings is a distortion of massive proportions. But it has immense rhetorical significance in American political debates and it spills over into political fault lines. On the whole, conservatives in contemporary America are thought to prefer the status quo, law and order, private property rights, markets, limited government, and a stratified society. Conversely, liberals are believed to prioritize big government (the legacy of F.D. Roosevelt's presidency in the 1930s), civil rights (the legacy of the 1960s), tolerance, and greater social equality. The accuracy of those generalizations aside, they pervade politics at every level, from tax policy, to immigration, to health insurance, to abortion. They create dichotomous confrontations that do not enable any form of common ground or mutual respect that liberal theorists would seek.

In a notable book entitled *The Decline of Liberalism as an Ideology*, the conservative American academic John H. Hallowell accused liberalism of moving from vigour to decadence. He held its tolerance and pluralism responsible for a sapping of the political and ideational will that eased the way for the interwar totalitarian ideologies of left and right. A more recent example of the unbalanced misrepresentation of liberalism occurred in the 1988 presidential campaign, focused in part on attacking the 'L-word', liberalism—described by one commentator as 'a deliberate attempt to remove the liberal tradition from America's political identity'. Michael Dukakis, the Democratic candidate, was 'tarred' with that brush, while liberalism was controversially equated with undermining national defence and leniency towards dangerous criminals. Unlike its European counterparts, the pejorative connotations of liberalism are strong enough in the USA to render the word tricky to employ favourably, and even its substitutes such as 'progressive' run into difficulties. Though there are recognizable liberal currents coursing through American politics, they relate to an ideology that all too often dares not speak its name.

Liberal excesses and arrogance

Liberalism did not invent the rule of law but it became its champion. Within the right package of values, the rule of law is an embodiment of good procedure, of fair treatment, of rights protection, and of the predictability needed to ensure the smooth running of a political system. But if the rule of law is divorced from democratic control—as was the case with British rule in India prior to 1947, and in other British colonies—what goes under the name of liberalism ceases to be liberal. Instead it becomes a strict, often repressive, imposition of law on a dominated society, without the quality of mercy, decency, or respect. Liberal standards of culture and education condemned colonial societies to an inferior status. Attempts of local societies to express dissent, to protest against imperial laws, or to follow their own practices were often quelled harshly. The free development of individuality, so cherished by liberals at home, did not apply to many cultures abroad. The greatest advocate of that triad, Mill, thought no differently, as the following passage shows (race was a people, a cultural and ethnic entity, in his terminology):

> ... we may leave out of consideration those backward states of society in which the race itself may be considered as in its nonage.... Despotism is a legitimate mode of government in dealing with barbarians, provided the end be their improvement.

In addition, the expansion of capitalism and of markets under the aegis of free trade does not hide the fact that they have frequently been employed as instruments of imperial dominion and exploitation, as Hobson knew. In the cases when so-called liberal states have been guilty of such exercises of power, they have excluded themselves from the liberal family, no matter what lip-service they may have paid to liberal ideals and visions. The fact that societies that were on the whole domestically liberal pursued shockingly illiberal policies abroad may then either be seen as the failed extension of an external liberal civilizing project or, more plausibly, simply as a deviation from the core beliefs of liberalism—chiefly from the universal claims to liberty and individual development it espouses.

In domestic policy, too, liberalism has had a fraught relationship with democracy, some of it justifiable, some not. From many points of view liberalism is an elite doctrine, catering to the educated, or maybe only those educated in a certain set of Western and Northern European values that then spread with uneven success to other corners of the globe. Liberalism lacks a populist appeal and cannot be delivered in easy slogans or sound bites. There is undoubtedly a visible paternalist streak among liberals—their high-mindedness, their self-belief in a civilizing mission, and their over-emphasis on education as the key to citizenship. Reading Mill's *On Liberty*, it is difficult not to assume that Mill regarded himself as a model for the free progressive individual he envisaged, remote from the experiences of the majority of people, about whose political capacities he had serious reservations. When one reads current political philosophers, the onerous requirement many of them endorse for people to reflect on and assess continuously their life-choices could only come from an intellectual's desk. No less notably, the more liberalism relies on regulatory measures to optimize the life-chances of all the members of a society, and the more it entertains a homogeneous and unified view of society, the more its directive tendencies come into play. That is evident especially in layer four liberalism, the layer that produced the welfare state with its parallel enabling and steering practices.

Liberalism's paternalism, with its professed benevolence of privileged classes towards the marginalized, is not of the hard kind, arrogant or overbearing by design. It is rather a soft paternalism driven by a genuine reforming urge. Nonetheless, throughout the 19th century and beyond, liberals promoted an idea of what a desirable character would look like and set preconditions for full participation in the growing democratic process. At first only property holders, then only those with minimal educational standards, were deemed fit for the full burdens of citizenship. Women fared even worse. In the UK, for example, they were excluded from full voting rights until 1928, including the years of the reforming liberal administrations between 1906 and 1914. One reason given was that they were insufficiently independent and their votes would be influenced by their fathers, brothers, and husbands—you cannot get more literally paternalist than that!

Having embraced democracy with initial reluctance, liberals sought to achieve social regeneration and establish benchmarks of what decent living would resemble, leaving many of those benchmarks to be determined by experts. Thus, individual contributions to social insurance schemes were made compulsory in order to render them financially viable. Many apparently liberal welfare policies, particularly in the USA, had punitive consequences for workers. American progressivism, too, was not exempt from paternalist traits, with Walter Lippmann extolling the importance of experts in relation to the general public in his book *Public Opinion*. There may be nothing wrong with putting one's trust in experts, provided they are under public scrutiny, but liberal policy-making tended to rush ahead of such consultation. Too many people were considered to be incapable of producing the social visions that could emancipate them. When UK Liberal governments introduced compulsory social insurance schemes over a century ago, they were resisted by older style, second and third layer liberals, as 'the newer Liberalism of Social Responsibility and... Paternal Government'. But other liberals saw that compulsion in a different light. The economist and politician L. Chiozza Money wrote:

> It is not difficult to get the average man who works for his living to see that the compulsion of democratic law is not only a different thing from the economic compulsion to which he must day by day

submit or starve, but that by virtue of the compulsion of law he may find mitigation of economic compulsion and even be saved from it.

Deliberate and inadvertent discrimination

Liberalism has its own silences and misrecognitions. If other ideologies often blatantly and deliberately tell a misleading tale about liberalism and its beliefs, liberals have themselves been guilty of walking around with blinkers and refusing to confront, or optimistically ignoring, crucial issues in their midst. Questions of race and ethnicity have only slowly crept into their field of vision in fifth layer liberalism. Liberal responsibility for their neglect cannot be overlooked, particularly in an ideology deeming itself to be socially aware and responsive. Even now liberalism exhibits a colour blindness it cannot completely shake off and its self-proclaimed inclusionary concern for the general interest has not eliminated an exclusionist, predominantly white, racial patriarchy.

Gender issues have been problematic for liberals in their own right, despite an earlier awareness of some of the problematics involved in the political standing of women, as illustrated by Mary Wollstonecraft. Mill, together with Harriet Taylor, his wife, was an early advocate of equal political rights—and votes—for women, insisting that 'the inequality of rights between men and women has no other source than the law of the strongest.' But the attainment of formal and legal equality that women's enfranchisement brought in its wake has been attacked by feminists on two grounds. First, it was too superficial and partial a reduction of inequality, as economic and cultural gender divides still obtained. Second, a theme common among recent feminists, it did little more than turn women politically into men, absorbing them into the already existing category of a citizen based on masculinist cultural characteristics, without any sensitivity towards constructive gender differences. That type of gender blindness doomed liberalism to fall short of feminist aspirations. Its historical association with contracts carried on to marriage with potentially oppressive practices. It was accused of falling prey to glib dichotomies in which men inhabited the public domain of mind, rationality, and universality, while women occupied the private domain of body, emotion, and particularity. Instead, feminists approached radical Marxist and postmodernist ideologies for more effective and more ethical solutions. Perspectives from outside the liberal camp tend, though, to exaggerate liberal ill-intent and incompetence, and some feminists have stereotyped all liberalisms with some of its early 20th century incarnations.

All these instances demonstrate how an ideology such as liberalism can falter the moment it pursues one of its core values or concepts in an extreme way, disregarding the others. Legal propriety without tolerance or regard for the general interest leads to institutional brutality. Unconstrained markets and wealth accumulation without social justice lead to profiteering and new unregulated concentrations of power. The search for civilized standards of living without democratic sensitivity leads to a remote elitism. The belief in rational consensus and national homogeneity without alertness to diversity and difference leads to social exclusion. The inclusion of women without recognizing the continuation of patriarchy by other means has proved inadequate. Any one liberal value on its own is no guarantee of liberalism and is more likely to undermine it. Liberalism as an ideology always has recourse to a set of values. It holds its various components in mutual check, balancing them out while allowing for flexible permutations as long as they are not self-destructing.

Liberal passions: a redemptive finale

Having noted some liberal lapses, this chapter ends with a corrective to a typical misidentification of the relationship of liberals to their creed. It is not in doubt that liberalism is about the rational application of reason to political issues. Yet in recent times that has often been costly in failing to find a language appealing to populations with different political tastes. The association of liberalism with cool, reflective rationality is only one side of the coin. Like any other ideology, liberalism has an emotional side that its critics underestimate and of which its adherents are not always aware. For Hobhouse, 'the philosophies that remain ineffectual and academic are those that are formed by abstract reflection without relation to the thirsty souls of human kind.' He contended that only the philosophies that arose out of the practical demands of human feeling have driving force. In effect, that is what gave them their ideological force. Liberalism was not just about reason but about imagination and social sentiment. That, liberals believe, is where one of liberalism's great strengths lies: its rational ideas—at their best—inspire passion and commitment. Liberals get hot under the collar when confronted with injustice, and outraged by violations of human dignity and by physical violence against people. Dehumanizing acts provoke anger and protest—though liberals being liberals, such protests usually occur through petitions, letters to the editor, and campaigns to change laws or policy, rather than by direct action. That is one reason, perhaps, why the suffragettes fighting for their right to vote over a century ago lost patience with liberalism. Liberal parties have been modest in their use of bombast and propaganda to arouse support in an age of mass politics, unlike demagogues from the left and the right. That, unfortunately, reduces their competitive edge in the world of politics.

Liberals, as we saw in Chapter 2, are not averse to nationalism either, though they may prefer its milder and less strident forms of patriotism. And nationalism is a very emotive practice of identifying with one's country or ethnicity. Liberals appear to extend the right to national self-determination to all nations, though in a world that acknowledges plural ethnic groupings it is increasingly complicated to agree on who constitutes a nation. Ultimately, liberals wax emotional about their own view of the world. As the Italian liberal historian Guido de Ruggiero put it, 'liberalism possesses that kind of tact or flair ... which ... is true political sensitiveness, and serves to recognize everything that is human—human strength and human weakness, human reason and human passion, human interest and human morality'. It is therefore fitting to end this book with Hobhouse's message to liberal democrats:

> ... they may come to learn that the vision of justice in the wholeness of her beauty kindles a passion that may not flare up into moments of dramatic scintillation, but burns with the enduring glow of the central heat.

References

Chapter 1: A house of many mansions

F. Fukuyama, *The End of History and the Last Man* (London: Penguin Books, 2012 [first published 1992]), especially pp. 45, 48, 51.

R.G. Collingwood, 'Introduction' in G. de Ruggiero, *The History of European Liberalism* (Boston: Beacon Press, 1959 [first published 1927]), p. vii.

L. Strauss, *Liberalism* (New York: Basic Books, 1968), p. vi.

L. Trilling, *The Liberal Imagination* (New York: Doubleday Anchor, 1954), p. 7.

L.T. Hobhouse, *Liberalism* (London: Williams and Norgate, 1911), pp. 46–7, 128. Hobhouse's *Liberalism* remains an exemplary exposition of the humanist liberal viewpoint.

K. Marx and F. Engels, *The German Ideology* (C.J. Arthur, ed.) (London: Lawrence and Wishart, 1970), p. 99.

C. Mouffe, *The Democratic Paradox* (London: Verso, 2000), p. 50.

R. Kirk, *The Conservative Mind* (London: Faber and Faber, 1954), pp. 388–9.

J. Rawls, *Lectures on the History of Political Philosophy* (Cambridge, MA: Harvard University Press, 2007), p. 12; and R. Dworkin, 'Liberalism' in R. Dworkin, *A Matter of Principle* (Clarendon Press: Oxford, 1986), pp. 191–2. These two highly prominent American philosophers of liberalism are discussed in Chapter 6.

John Maynard Keynes was the most influential economist of the twentieth century and also a supporter of the British Liberal Party. The quotation comes from his *Essays in Persuasion* (London: Macmillan and Co., 1931), p. 343.

Chapter 2: The liberal narrative

John Locke's seminal discussions of consent and of resistance are in his 'Second Treatise of Government', *Two Treatises of Government* (Cambridge: Cambridge University Press, 1963), Sections 96, 119, 225.

Isaiah Berlin's singular take on Machiavelli's *The Prince* is in I. Berlin, *Against the Current* (London: The Hogarth Press, 1979), pp. 25–79.

É. Durkheim, *The Division of Labour in Society* (New York: The Free Press, 1964).

Mill quoted W. von Humboldt's *The Limits of State Action* (Cambridge: Cambridge University Press, 1969), p. 48. This was only published in English in 1854, a few years before Mill's *On Liberty* in 1859.

H. Croly, *Progressive Democracy* (New Brunswick: Transaction Publications, 1914), pp. 203–4.

L. Hartz, *The Liberal Tradition in America* (New York: Harcourt, Brace and World, 1955), p. 228.

L. von Mises, *Liberalism* (Irvington, NY, 1985 [first published 1927]), pp. xvi–xvii.

H. Spencer, *The Man versus the State* (Harmondsworth: Penguin Books, 1969 [first published 1884]), p. 67.

Chapter 3: Layers of liberalism

Reinhart Koselleck's approach is epitomized in his *Futures Past* (Cambridge, MA: MIT Press, 1985).

J. Locke, 'Second Treatise of Government', *Two Treatises of Government* (Cambridge: Cambridge University Press, 1963), Section 57.

C.B. Macpherson, *The Political Theory of Possessive Individualism* (Oxford: Clarendon Press, 1962).

John Bright, Speech on 'Foreign Policy' in Birmingham, 29 October 1858. http://oll.libertyfund.org/titles/bright-selected-speeches-of-the-rt-hon-john-bright-m-p-on-public-questions#lf0618_label_037

The quotation from a speech by Richard Cobden at Manchester, 15 January 1846 is in A. Bullock and M. Shock (eds.), *The Liberal Tradition from Fox to Keynes* (Oxford: Clarendon Press, 1956), p. 53.

The quotation from John Milton's *Areopagitica* (1644) can be found in http://cdn.preterhuman.net/texts/literature/books_in_PDF/1644%20Areopagitica.pdf, p. 36.

William Beveridge's five giants are listed in his report, 'Social Insurance and Allied Services', Cmd 6404 (London: His Majesty's Stationery Office, 1942), p. 6.

The phrase 'muscular liberalism' appears in a speech by the British Prime Minister, David Cameron, delivered in Munich on 5 February 2011. See http://www.newstatesman.com/blogs/the-staggers/2011/02/terrorism-islam-ideology

George W. Bush, 'Speech to the World Affairs Council of Philadelphia', Philadelphia, Pennsylvania, 12 December 2005. http://www.presidentialrhetoric.com/speeches/12.12.05.html

Chapter 4: The morphology of liberalism

For a detailed discussion of liberal morphology, and ideological morphology in general, see M. Freeden, *Ideologies and Political Theory: A Conceptual Approach* (Oxford: Clarendon Press, 1996). A briefer guide is M. Freeden, *Ideology: A Very Short Introduction* (Oxford: Oxford University Press, 2003).

J. Locke, 'Second Treatise of Government', *Two Treatises of Government* (Cambridge: Cambridge University Press, 1963), Section 5.

B. Mandeville, *The Fable of the Bees or Private Vices, Publick Benefits*. http://lf-oll.s3.amazonaws.com/titles/846/Mandeville_0014-01_EBk_v6.0.pdf

L. Hartz, *The Liberal Tradition in America* (New York: Harcourt, Brace and World, 1955), p. 9.

D. Bell, 'What is Liberalism?' *Political Theory*, vol. 42 (2014), pp. 682–715. This is a considered attempt to reinterpret the history of liberal thinking as the sum of the arguments that liberals claim to be liberal over time and space, while Bell abstains from assessing their relative weight within the liberal tradition.

Chapter 5: Liberal luminaries

J.S. Mill, 'On Liberty' in J.M. Robson (ed.), *Essays on Politics and Society, Collected Works of J.S. Mill*, vol. 18 (Toronto: University of Toronto Press, Routledge and Kegan Paul, 1977), p. 261.

T.H. Green, *Liberal Legislation and Freedom of Contract* (Oxford: Slatter and Rose, 1881), pp. 9–10.

L.T. Hobhouse, *Liberalism* (London: Williams and Norgate, 1911), pp. 124, 126.

J.A. Hobson, *The Crisis of Liberalism* (London: P.S. King & Son, 1911), pp. xii, 97, 113.

M. Wollstonecraft, *A Vindication of the Rights of Woman* (Harmondsworth: Penguin Books, 1975 [first published 1792]), pp. 139, 319.

B. Constant, 'The Liberty of the Ancients Compared with that of the Moderns' in *Political Writings* (B. Fontana ed.), (Cambridge: Cambridge University Press, 1988), pp. 317, 323.

W. von Humboldt, *The Limits of State Action* (Cambridge: Cambridge University Press, 1969), p. 10, and J.S. Mill, 'On Liberty', *op. cit.*, p. 261.

B. Croce, *Politics and Morals* (London: George Allen and Unwin, 1946), pp. 78, 84, 87, 102.

C. Rosselli, *Liberal Socialism* (Princeton, NJ: Princeton University Press, 1994 [first published 1930]), pp. 78, 85, 86.

J. Dewey, *Liberalism and Social Action* (New York: G.P. Putnam's Sons, 1935), pp. 15–16, 27, 38, 43. Dewey's book remains one of the finest reflections on liberal values and liberal history.

F.A. Hayek, 'Liberalism' in F.A. Hayek (ed.), *New Studies in Philosophy, Politics, Economics and the History of Ideas* (London: Routledge & Kegan Paul, 1978), pp. 130, 141, 148; F.A. Hayek, *The Constitution of Liberty* (London: Routledge & Kegan Paul, 1960), p. 39.

Chapter 6: Philosophical liberalism: idealizing justice

John Rawls, *A Theory of Justice* (Oxford: Oxford University Press, 1971), p. 3. He discusses the idea of a realistic utopia in J. Rawls, *The Law of Peoples* (Cambridge, MA: Harvard University Press, 1999), pp. 11–23. On Rawls's minimalist liberalism, see J. Rawls, *Political Liberalism* (New York: Columbia University Press, 1996).

Herbert Asquith's comment on individual development is in a speech he delivered in the House of Commons (*Hansard*, 4th Series, 18 April 1907).

For the views of Rawls and Dworkin on neutrality, see J. Rawls, *Political Liberalism*, *op. cit.*, p. 161; and R. Dworkin, 'Liberalism' in R. Dworkin, *A Matter of Principle* (Clarendon Press: Oxford, 1986), pp. 181–204.

H. Croly, *The Promise of American Life* (New York: Macmillan, 1909), p. 192.
G.F. Gaus, *Justificatory Liberalism* (Oxford: Oxford University Press, 1996), pp. 293–4.
B. Williams, *In the Beginning was the Deed* (Princeton: Princeton University Press, 2005), especially pp. 1–18.
I. Berlin, *Four Essays on Liberty* (Oxford: Oxford University Press, 1969).
This contains his most famous analyses of liberal thought and his treatment of the concept of liberty.

Chapter 7: Misappropriations, disparagements, and lapses

J. Szacki, *Liberalism after Communism* (Budapest: Central European University Press, 1995), p. 109.
G. Sørensen, *A Liberal World Order in Crisis* (Ithaca, NY: Cornell University Press, 2011), p. 54.
R.H. Tawney, *Equality* (London: George Allen & Unwin, 1938 edn), p. 208.
H.J. Laski, *The Rise of European Liberalism* (London: Unwin Books, 1962 [1936]), pp. 167–8.
J.H. Hallowell, *The Decline of Liberalism as an Ideology* (Berkeley, CA: University of California Press, 1943).
The comment on the 1988 presidential campaign is in P.M. Garry, *Liberalism and American Identity* (Kent, Ohio: Kent State University Press, 1992), p. 10.
J.S. Mill, 'On Liberty', in J.M. Robson (ed.), *Essays on Politics and Society, Collected Works of J.S. Mill*, vol. 18 (Toronto: University of Toronto Press, Routledge and Kegan Paul, 1977), p. 224.
W. Lippmann, *Public Opinion* (New York: Macmillan, 1922).
J. Armsden, 'First Principles of Social Reform', *Westminster Review*, vol. 169 (1908), p. 639.
L. Chiozza Money, *Insurance versus Poverty* (London: Methuen and Co, 1912), p. 7.
J.S. Mill, 'The Subjection of Women', in J.M. Robson (ed.), *Essays on Equality, Law and Education, Collected Works of J.S. Mill*, vol. 21 (Toronto: University of Toronto Press, Routledge and Kegan Paul, 1984), p. 264.
L.T. Hobhouse, *Liberalism* (London: Williams and Norgate, 1911), pp. 51, 250–1.
G. de Ruggiero, *The History of European Liberalism* (Boston: Beacon Press, 1959 [1927]), p. 390.

Further reading

Chapter 1: A house of many mansions

There are more works on liberalism than anyone could reasonably be expected to consult. For older but still influential histories of liberalism, see G. de Ruggiero, *The History of European Liberalism* (Boston: Beacon Press, 1959 [first published 1927]; and L. Hartz, *The Liberal Tradition in America* (New York: Harcourt, Brace and World, 1955). Instructive studies are by J.G. Merquior, *Liberalism Old and New* (Boston: Twayne Publishers, 1991); J.A. Hall, *Liberalism* (London: Paladin, 1988); and R. Bellamy, *Liberalism and Modern Society* (Cambridge: Polity Press, 1992). An excellent analysis in the American context is P. Starr, *Freedom's Power: The True Force of Liberalism* (New York: Basic Books, 2007). For a recent account, see Edmund Fawcett, *Liberalism: The Life of an Idea* (Princeton: Princeton University Press, 2014). For a highly critical discussion of the historical failings of liberalism, see D. Losurdo, *Liberalism: A Counter-History* (London: Verso, 2011).

The best philosophical study of liberal ideology still is L.T. Hobhouse, *Liberalism* (London: Williams and Norgate, 1911).

The lodestars of the American philosophical approach to liberalism are a book and a chapter, respectively: J. Rawls, *Political Liberalism* (New York: Columbia University Press, 1996); and R. Dworkin, 'Liberalism' in R. Dworkin, *A Matter of Principle* (Clarendon Press: Oxford, 1986). An important early critique of Rawls is M. Sandel, *Liberalism and the Limits of Justice* (Cambridge: Cambridge University Press, 1982).

On the nature of ideological morphology, see M. Freeden, *Ideology: A Very Short Introduction* (Oxford, 2003); and the chapters on 'The Morphological Analysis of Ideology' and on 'Liberalism' in M. Freeden, L.T. Sargent, and M. Stears (eds.), *The Oxford Handbook of Political Ideologies* (Oxford: Oxford University Press, 2013).

On liberal feminism and its critique, see S. Moller Okin, *Justice, Gender and the Family* (New York: Basic Books, 1989); and A.M. Jaggar, *Feminist Politics and Human Nature* (Totowa, NJ: Rowman and Littlefield, 1983).

Chapter 2: The liberal narrative

An instructive introduction to Machiavelli's republicanism is Q. Skinner, *Machiavelli* (Oxford: Oxford University Press, 1981). Though no proto-liberal himself, features of Machiavelli's republicanism and endorsement of a civic-minded participatory society percolated into 20th century liberal discourses. See also Q. Skinner, *Liberty before Liberalism* (Cambridge: Cambridge University Press, 1998).

For contrasting British liberal views on private property, see R. Muir, *The New Liberalism* (London: The Daily News Ltd, n.d. [1923]) and J.A. Hobson, *Property and Improperty* (London: Victor Gollanz, 1937).

For an examination of Durkheim's liberalism, see W. Logue, *From Philosophy to Sociology: The Evolution of French Liberalism 1890–1914* (Dekalb, IL: Northern Illinois University Press, 1983).

On the British Liberal Party in the 19th century, see W. Lyon Blease, *A Short History of English Liberalism* (London: T. Fisher Unwin, 1913).

The clearest expression of Jeremy Bentham's utilitarian individualism is his *An Introduction to the Principles of Morals and Legislation* (New York: Dover Publications, 2007).

G.W.F. Hegel's magisterial work on ethical and political philosophy is his *Elements of the Philosophy of Right* (Cambridge: Cambridge University Press, 1991).

G. Mazzini's exhortation to patriotism can be found in his *The Duties of Man* (London: Chapman and Hall, 1862).

On the importance of society in new liberal understandings, see J.A. Hobson, *The Social Problem* (London: James Nisbet & Co. 1901).

The relevance of social evolution to liberal arguments is explored in D.G. Ritchie, *Darwinism and Politics* (London: Swan Sonnenschein, 1901); and L.T. Hobhouse, *Social Evolution and Political Theory* (New York: Columbia University Press, 1911).

For analyses of British social liberalism, see M. Freeden, *The New Liberalism: An Ideology of Social Reform* (Clarendon Press: Oxford, 1978); and M. Freeden, *Liberalism Divided: A Study in British Political Thought 1914–1939* (Clarendon Press: Oxford University Press, 1986).

Chapter 3: Layers of liberalism

For north European liberal variants, see I.K. Lakaniemi, A. Rotkirch, and H. Stenius (eds.), *Liberalism—Seminars in Historical and Political Keywords in Northern Europe* (Helsinki: Renvall Institute, 1995).

On the incorporation of time and temporality into liberal thought, see M. Freeden, *Liberal Languages: Ideological Imaginations and Twentieth Century Political Thought* (Princeton, NJ: Princeton University Press, 2005), chapter 1.

For probing treatments of imperialism, see J. Darwin, *Unfinished Empire: The Global Expansion of Britain* (London: Penguin Books, 2012); H.C.G. Matthew, *The Liberal Imperialists* (Oxford: Oxford University Press, 1973); D. Chakrabarty, *Provincializing Europe: Postcolonial Thought and Historical Difference* (Princeton, NJ: Princeton University Press, 2000).

For the politics of identity and difference, see I.M. Young, *Justice and the Politics of Difference* (Princeton, NJ: Princeton University Press, 1990); A.T. Baumeister, *Liberalism and the 'Politics of Difference'* (Edinburgh: Edinburgh University Press, 2000).

On liberalism in India, see R. Bhargava, *The Promise of India's Secular Democracy* (New Delhi: Oxford University Press, 2010); R. Bajpai, *Debating Difference: Group Rights and Liberal Democracy in India* (New Delhi: Oxford University Press, 2011).

On liberalism in the Netherlands, see H. Te Velde, 'The Organization of Liberty: Dutch Liberalism as a Case of the History of European Constitutional Liberalism', *European Journal of Political Theory*, vol. 7 (2008), pp. 65–79.

On liberal approaches to the wearing of headscarves, see C. Laborde, *Critical Republicanism: The Hijab Controversy and Political Philosophy* (Oxford: Oxford University Press, 2008); and

K.A. Beydoun, '*Laïcité*, Liberalism, and the Headscarf', *Journal of Islamic Law and Culture*, vol. 10 (2008), pp. 191–215.

Chapter 4: The morphology of liberalism

On essentially contested concepts, see W.B. Gallie, 'Essentially Contested Concepts', *Proceedings of the Aristotelian Society*, vol. 56 (1955–6), pp. 167–98; and D. Collier, F.D. Hidalgo, and A.O. Maciuceanu, 'Essentially Contested Concepts: Debates and Applications', *Journal of Political Ideologies*, vol. 11 (2006), pp. 211–46.

On liberal ideas and concepts, see W.A. Galston, *Liberal Purposes* (Cambridge: Cambridge University Press, 1991); S. Macedo, *Liberal Virtues* (Oxford: Clarendon Press, 1991); and G.F. Gaus, *Political Concepts and Political Theories* (Boulder, CO: Westview Press, 2000).

On comparative liberal themes, see M. Freeden, 'European Liberalisms: An Essay in Comparative Political Thought', *European Journal of Political Theory*, vol. 7 (2008), pp. 9–30.

Chapter 5: Liberal luminaries

Further reading on the thinkers in this chapter can be explored through many of the introductory books listed for Chapter 1.

Two sources for Max Weber's thought are H.H. Gerth and C.W. Mills (eds.), *From Max Weber* (New York: Oxford University Press, 1946); and P. Lassman and R. Speirs (eds.), *Weber: Political Writings* (Cambridge: Cambridge University Press, 1994).

Chapter 6: Philosophical liberalism: idealizing justice

An illuminating exposition of liberal egalitarianism is in A. Gutmann, *Liberal Equality* (Cambridge University Press, 1980).

There is an extensive literature on the liberal-communitarian divide. For different views, see M. Sandel, *Liberalism and the Limits of Justice* (Cambridge: Cambridge University Press, 1982); S. Mulhall and A. Swift, *Liberals and Communitarians* (Oxford: Blackwells, 1996); and C. Taylor, 'Cross-Purposes: The Liberal-Communitarian Debate' in N.L. Rosenblum (ed.), *Liberalism and the Moral Life* (Cambridge, MA: Harvard University Press, 1989), pp. 159–82.

For investigations of liberal neutrality, see R.E. Goodin and A. Reeve (eds.), *Liberal Neutrality* (London: Routledge, 1989); and W. Kymlicka, 'Liberal Individualism and Liberal Neutrality', *Ethics*, vol. 99 (1989), pp. 883–905.

On ranking as a political act, see M. Freeden, *The Political Theory of Political Thinking: The Anatomy of a Practice* (Oxford: Oxford University Press, 2013), pp. 132–65.

On Berlin's pluralism, see G. Crowder, *Liberalism and Value Pluralism* (London: Continuum, 2002); J. Cherniss, *A Mind and its Time: The Development of Isaiah Berlin's Political Thought* (Oxford: Oxford University Press, 2013); G. Garrard, 'The Counter-Enlightenment Liberalism of Isaiah Berlin', *Journal of Political Ideologies*, vol. 2 (1997), pp. 281–96; and G.E. Gaus, *Contemporary Theories of Liberalism* (London: Sage Publications, 2003).

Chapter 7: Misappropriations, disparagements, and lapses

On neoliberalism, see M. Steger and R.K. Roy, *Neoliberalism: A Very Short Introduction* (Oxford: Oxford University Press, 2010); and M. Olssen, *Liberalism, Neoliberalism, Social Democracy* (Abingdon: Routledge, 2010). See also M. Thatcher and V. Schmidt (eds.), *Resilient Liberalism in Europe's Political Economy* (Cambridge: Cambridge University Press, 2013), especially the chapters by the editors, A. Gamble, and M. Ferrera.

On East European liberalism, see Z. Suda and J. Musil (eds.), *The Meaning of Liberalism: East and West* (Budapest: Central European University Press, 2000).

On liberal internationalism, see B. Jahn, *Liberal Internationalism* (Houndmills, Basingstoke: Palgrave Macmillan, 2013).

For illiberal excesses, see D. King, *In the Name of Liberalism: Illiberal Social Policy in the USA and Britain* (Oxford: Oxford University Press, 1999).

On liberal paternalism, see M. Freeden, 'Democracy and Paternalism: The Struggle over Shaping British Liberal Welfare Thinking', in A. Kessler-Harris and M. Vaudagna (eds.), *Democracy and Social Rights in the 'Two Wests'* (Torino: Otto, 2009), pp. 107–22; and W. Lippman, *Public Opinion* (New York: Brace and Co., 1922).

On the gender oppressiveness of liberal contract, see C. Pateman, *The Sexual Contract* (Cambridge: Polity Press, 1988).

Index

E

F

G

H

I

J

K

L

M

N

O

P

R

SOCIAL MEDIA
Very Short Introduction

Join our community

www.oup.com/vsi

- Join us online at the official Very Short Introductions **Facebook** page.
- Access the thoughts and musings of our authors with our online **blog**.
- Sign up for our monthly **e-newsletter** to receive information on all new titles publishing that month.
- Browse the full range of Very Short Introductions online.
- Read **extracts** from the Introductions for free.
- Visit our library of **Reading Guides**. These guides, written by our expert authors will help you to question again, why you think what you think.
- If you are a teacher or lecturer you can order inspection copies quickly and simply via our website.